# The Road Behind Me

# The Road Behind Me

*(The Lie of Hannah)*

*A Memoir*

*RjCook*

Published 2016 by Creativia
Paperback design by Creativia (www.creativia.org)
ISBN: 978-1532919237
Cover art by http://www.thecovercollection.com/

*With thanks to*

*…Patti, the love of my life,*

*for her tolerance and support.*

*…my children, for giving me the*

*greatest memories any man can hope for.*

*…"Bing", for his enduring friendship.*

*…Hannah, wherever she may be.*

# Contents

# Prologue
# Framing the Lie

*When I was young, I wished for you,*
*and just in time, my wish came true.*
*Then I wished that it could be*
*how I loved you, your love for me.*
*But soon I wished it wasn't so,*
*wishing that you wouldn't go.*

In the summer of 1974, I ventured from the little suburban town in northern New Jersey where I was raised, to Anaheim, California, then back again a year later, hitchhiking most of the way. This story is about my life's journey both before and during that memorable trek, why that sojourn was not by choice, but out of necessity, and the amazing adventures life presented to me along the way. It is also about the lie that put me on the road, the reason the lie existed at all, and how it caused heartache that I dealt with during each event I experienced. Mostly, it is a story of unrequited love and the lengths to which a man would go to vanquish the demons of painful memories.

## The Years behind Me
**1952**

- *Dwight Eisenhower elected President of the United States*

- *Jonas Salk develops Polio vaccine*

- *"Your Cheatin' Heart" by Hank Williams is released*

- *Microwave ovens are made available for domestic use with the first models being the size of refrigerators and costing more than $1,200.*

- *I am born in Passaic, New Jersey on a warm summer day.*

**1953**

- *Nikita Khrushchev wins power struggle in Soviet Union after the death of Josef Stalin*

- *An expedition led by Sir Edmund Hillary is the first to reach the summit of Mount Everest*

- *"Doggie in the Window" by Patti Page is released*

- *TV Guide debuts; on the cover of the first issue are Lucille Ball and her newborn son, Desi Arnaz IV*

- *Hannah is born in Hackensack, NJ on a warm summer day.*

# Chapter One
# The Early Road

It's been said that a man falls in love an average of three times in his life. If that is an accurate assessment, then it stands to reason that two of those three must end in heartbreak. Over the lifetime of an average man, I would guess that's not the worst statistic we have to endure, but I was one of the unlucky fellows who had the misfortune of experiencing two of my allotted three heartaches before the age of twenty, both within the same year separated by only a few months.

Though this is mostly a story of my odyssey from the summer of 1974 to the summer of 1975, it could not be told unless I explained what the shattered heart beating in the chest of a young man brought about, how I lived a lie that affected only me, yet I still continued to act out this falsehood with those who knew me. To this day, so many years later, some of them remember why I journeyed to America's left coast the way I want them to remember it.

My life, as best I can determine, began at a later date than what my family would tell you. They would assert that I was born in June of 1952 in a hospital in Passaic, New Jersey, but I will tell you that just happened to be the time my mother gave birth to me. I was the youngest of six, four girls and two boys, all of them half-siblings. My sisters and brother were all out of the house by the time I was five, having married, joined the army or, in two of my sister's cases, having moved back to their natural mother's home. I did remain close to three of them: Joan (a loving, wonderful woman who passed away far too early), Peggy (who was the oldest of the girls) and my brother Bruce who was my mother's son by a previous relationship before my father. My heritage is unclear: Dutch, German, Irish, and Native-American. I was a potpourri of them all. Basically, I am a mutt with no clear lineage, but you are what you are and what you become. As it is with most middle-class mixed lineage children of my generation, I could tell you my grandparents' names, but the names of their parents remain a mystery to me. I couldn't even recount my mother's father's name, and the only reason I know her mother's is because, at Mom's suggestion, my youngest daughter was christened for her. Some cultures can give you the names of all of their ancestors, going back quite a bit in time. I couldn't even identify all of my cousins from my father's side unless they were wearing name tags.

My mother's father was one of several men her mother married, or kept company with, to ensure her children survived during the lean years of the Great Depression. To this day, I have no idea how large a family my mother actually came from because there were aunts and uncles showing up periodically throughout my life. People whom I'd never met before, several decidedly older than Mom, told me they were my mother's brother or sister. Both of my grandparents from my mother's side were gone well before I came onto the scene, but I do recall a picture of my grandmother that Mom kept on my dresser when I was very young. I was terrified of this portrait of my maternal grandmother, so stern and serious with eyes that seemed to follow me wherever I was in the room. I would lay the picture down at night, which would upset Mom. She would tell me that her mother was such a loving woman and would have worshipped me, but those were hollow words to a five-year-old who was frightened of an image he didn't understand.

Dad's family was more stable but equally as large. I know of six girls and three boys but have been told there might have been a few that didn't survive childbirth. Both his parents lived until I was into my late twenties, but I never came to know them that well; that seemed to be reserved for my girl cousins. My father's grandfather from his mother's side was a Civil War veteran, a fact confirmed by several documents someone in the family holds. He also opened the very first dry cleaners the city of Passaic, New Jersey ever saw. Dad's memory of his grandfather was vague; he recalled only that he was wheelchair-bound near the end of his days and was very difficult to understand when he spoke.

Dad often told me stories of how they struggled to survive during the Depression years, so many of them living all together in a small apartment on a dead-end street in Passaic. Some married just to escape the confines of what must have seemed like a God-appointed condemnation, or, from what I've been told, a tyrannical, heavy-drinking father. What bearing did all this have on me? *Nothing*, except to give you an idea of the gene pool that eventually produced me.

The 'me' that I've come to recognize didn't surface until many years after my birth. I had survived a confusing, often lonely, often bewildering childhood. It was difficult to establish any enduring friendships because we moved from one apartment to the next until we settled in a single-family home my parents bought from my aunt. Since all of my siblings had long since moved on, getting to know them was piece-meal, gradient over time. I established bonds particularly with Joan, Peggy and Bruce, over a period of years with geography playing a factor because we were so transient. My younger years also found me entertaining not one, not two, but *five* child psychologists with my original sci-fi short stories and active imagination. My parents, desperately seeking an answer to their dysfunctional marriage, had put the blame on my "peculiar" tastes to explain why they didn't work together. In the long run, they did work, maybe not as happy as they could have been, but nonetheless they had nearly sixty years together before Mom passed quietly in her bed at home after ten-years of being debilitated by a stroke, all the while my father tending to her every need. Was it enough to earn his place in the good side of the afterlife? Maybe, but he certainly had his share of atonement due.

We weren't a particularly religious family; in fact, while Mom attended church on special occasions, I have no memory of Dad ever stepping foot inside any place Holy unless it was a wedding or similar event. I was baptized in the Episcopalian Church of St John's in Passaic, New Jersey, and only through the courtesy of my uncles who would pick me up and drop me back home was Sunday service a regular in my life. I ran the gamut of candle-bearer to master of ceremonies during that tenure, but it wasn't enough to solidify my belief in an All-Mighty Entity. From the early age of eleven or twelve, when my church-going days ended, I had doubts concerning the hereafter. There were phases - Buddhism, Krishna Conscientiousness, Eastern mysticism - but not one held my ardor for any measurable length of time. Thinking back, I wonder if maybe faith would have eased my journey going forward, but overall faith just didn't do it for me. If God existed, I thought, He was a cruel Being lacking compassion. In the big picture, I didn't allow my stinted forays into any religious doctrine to occupy my thoughts and deeds. I moseyed on through life doing all the things that boys do in suburban New Jersey, but when I turned sixteen there was an awakening within me that bellowed for recognition. The world was suddenly larger than I imagined and it was time to stake my claim.

## The Years behind Me
**1968**

- *Martin Luther King, Jr. assassinated in Memphis, Tennessee*

- *Sirhan Sirhan shoots Bobby Kennedy at the Ambassador Hotel in Los Angeles, California. Bobby Kennedy dies the next morning from his wounds*

- *The New York Jets win AFL championship*

- *Beatles release their White Album*

**1969**

- *The New York Jets win Super Bowl III*

- *Apollo 11 astronauts Neil Armstrong and Edwin Aldrin become the first humans to walk on the moon.*

- *Charles Manson orchestrates the senseless murders of 7 people in two nights in Los Angeles*

- *400,000 people gather for the Woodstock Festival in Bethel, New York on Max Yasgur's farm*

- *The Festival at Altamont Raceway in California ends with the tragic death of Meredith Hunter at the hands of Hell's Angels, essentially bringing to an end the peace-love attitude of the 1960's*

**1971**

- *Twenty-sixth Amendment to US Constitution lowers voting age to 18*

- *Patton wins Oscar for best picture*

- *Jim Morrison dies in Paris at 27 years of age*

- *The cost of a first-class stamp goes from .06 cents to .08 cents.*

- *Idi Amin seizes power in Uganda*

# Chapter Two
# Recognizing Love

It was 1968, a year after the "Summer of Love." Bobby Kennedy and Martin Luther King had recently been murdered, the Vietnam War was the nightmare of most American males in their late teens, the Beatles were still together, and eight-track tapes were still in the future. I was a skinny sixteen-year-old, nothing much to look at, and with hair far too long according to every adult in my world. Insecurity was the order of the day for me. I was a barely skilled novice musician dreaming of rock stardom, having friends with the same aspirations and the same level of skill. We were trapped in the suburban world of a total vacuous New Jersey town nine miles west of New York City. With that city's noble skyline in our view, our summer days were spent in idle wandering from my house to their house and back again, listening to the latest vinyl records by the Beatles, Rolling Stones, the Who, Jefferson Airplane; far too many great bands to list. When not sitting around someone's record player, reading the album jackets while the music enveloped us, we occasionally would sidetrack to a local park until we were told to move on along by either boredom or the local law. It was around this time that Peggy left to live in California, a move I didn't quite understand why but would become clearer to me in time to come. My initial emotion was one of envy, and I was the guy with the cool sister who went to live in California when it was considered a legendary land of hippies, Haight-Ashbury, and great music in the 1960's.

We also found a playground just around the corner from where I lived that proved a convenient retreat that included girls our age working for the town's Parks Department, tending to children coloring, gluing Popsicle sticks, and working with construction paper. Normally, this would have been a mind-numbing way to spend an afternoon, but did I mention that girls our age worked there? That was cause enough to dispel any chance of boredom to a sixteen-year-old boy.

Sixteen-year-old boys, especially when I was that age, were so much less mature than any sixteen-year-old girls I knew. We exposed ourselves to ostentatious displays of bravado and showing-off that sometimes drew smiles, or even a laugh, but we still left the playground each day in a testosterone-filled companionship that had us convincing each other that, sure, I think she likes me, maybe I will ask her out; yeah, tomorrow I'll do it. Yet each night alone in our beds, masturbation was the order of the moment as we envisioned our hoped-to-be girlfriends in all the carnal imagery we could muster.

It was on July 2nd of 1968 as I was sitting on one of the playground benches under a canopy that I realized I was receiving special attention from one very attractive young lady employed there. She was a real Irish stunner with long, red hair and freckled, flawless features. Despite all of that, I mostly remember her voice at that moment. It was silky and smooth, soft yet clear, with a gentle tone that made me believe maybe something was happening here. Shelly was a beauty in anyone's world, but my insecurity about myself still prompted me to have my friend Pat convince me that, yes, she was worth pursuing.

"What do you think?" I asked him. "Does she like me? You think she's good looking?" I rambled inanely to my confused friend who was baffled by even the consideration this beautiful young woman was anything but, and he told me in no uncertain terms that I was never going to do better. It wasn't that I didn't already know the answers, but my fear of failure and rejection was looking for a way out before

I found the way in. Or was I preparing a defense if my efforts to court Shelly failed?

Shelly did fall for me and I for her, fast and hard – and, as is my wont, I was head over heels in love almost immediately. This was both a habit and a problem I dealt with my entire life when it came to women. Having come from a family that never expressed emotion and certainly never said it out loud; when these emotions were introduced into my life, it was candy to a baby. Shelly was the first woman I ever passionately kissed, the first I said *I love you* to and who returned the sentiment, and the first woman I ever made love to. Because of Shelly, love was new in my world and it was wonderful!

We were young and in love but, unfortunately, too young to be in love. Our relationship was doomed to failure by so many distractions, like our youth, her parents (I'll never forget the look of horror on her mother's face when she brought me home for the first time), her maturity compared to mine … and finally, Shelly's being sent off to school to make a life for herself that didn't include me. It was a calculated move precipitated by her parents, ensuring her future through the benefits of a highly respected college and creating distance between us that they knew would prove too difficult to maintain a relationship. To them, I was local fodder, too blue collar to be worthy of their daughter. Unfortunately, they were right.

Our time together lasted the better part of one year and nine months, with eight of those months finding Shelly away at school. During that time, my group of friends expanded, mostly including fellow musicians or artists, and within that group I met Mary. Mary also had red hair, was also Irish (which seemed to be the type of women I was predisposed to), and so cute! This was new territory: I was still in a relationship with Shelly, albeit long distance and weakening a bit every day. My insecurities with women were a thing of the past, and the concept of "cheating" was too great a temptation for an eighteen-year-old to resist. Mary knew I was already involved with someone else but didn't seem to mind, so we began a relationship that was put aside with each trip home from school by Shelly. In full view of our friends, who were also Shelly's friends, I played the dedicated boyfriend while Mary lingered nearby, awaiting her turn to be with me each time Shelly returned to school. I was living the high life of love. And don't believe for a moment that our mutual friends were not aware of Mary and me being together. We never hid our passion towards each other those weeks Shelly was gone, but why they simply accepted it, or tolerated it, I never knew and odds are I wouldn't have cared much anyway. I had two beautiful women and such a clear conscience. As long as I was careful, what could go wrong? But even then, being so young, I knew the dam would eventually break.

It did, on Good Friday, April 9th, 1971. I called on Shelly, who was home from school on Easter break. I paid my respects to her family before we left and walked back to my house. The sun was shining, it was a beautiful spring day, but something was amiss, I could sense it but I was at a loss as to why Shelly seemed so distant. We stood in my parents' dining room on opposite sides of the table; from where I stood I could see my mother working in the yard. I asked Shelly what was wrong but received no reply, instead there was an icy silence. I was determined to learn what was bothering her, what was keeping her mind elsewhere, and why she was here with me only physically. My memory after all these years won't let me tell you exactly how the next few moments evolved, but I do remember going to kiss her, only for her to turn her head away. In that moment of total exasperation my world went blank; I could feel the unexpected flush on my face, the assault of fear and worry. I asked Shelly if she loved me anymore, dreading to hear what I might hear.

Tearfully, she replied, "No, I'm sorry…no, I don't."

I was suddenly cast into a vacuum of despair; there was begging, pleading, and tears on my part. I kept my eyes on my mother, hoping she remained in the yard so my display of a broken man was only between me and the woman I loved but just lost. If you've been through this pain, then you can understand why there aren't any words outside of songs of lost love, or sonnets to broken hearts that could ever accurately describe the agony I was feeling as my whole world came crashing down unmercifully. Somehow I agreed to her plea that we should remain friends, that there was nothing more to be said, and I walked her home. Though only two blocks, it was one of the longest walks I'd ever taken. My heart was beating so hard, the world made no sense, I made no sense. Life was a trap, and I was caught hopelessly in its snare. Khalil Gibran wrote, "Ever has it been that love knows not its own depth until the hour of separation." My hour had arrived: Shelly was the very first woman who broke my heart, and those words could not have been more poignant.

Now here is the where the seeds of my great lie were sown, and why my deception eventually became necessary: I wore the pain of Shelly's loss on my sleeve. I cried to my closest friends, especially Pat and Mike, and to my not-so-close friends, to Mary, who I was still dating, and anyone else who would tolerate me. I was a sorry and pathetic figure of a shattered teenager who clung to the hope that I could have the woman I loved back in my life if only I could see her, talk to her, show her I could change and had great plans for the future.

But none of those things happened. None were true. I wrote to her at school, letters upon letters that were never directly to the point about my splintered soul lest I should discourage her from ever replying, which she always did but never more than words from a friend. For a short time afterwards, Shelly would join me and our friends when she was home from college, but that didn't work out at all. I couldn't be in the same room with her and not make a total fool of myself, making her uncomfortable. Eventually she stopped calling completely. Shelly was gone forever, and I was convinced my pain was forever as well. Why Mary hung around after my piteous displays, I never knew. Such fools we are in love, whether having won or lost our heart's desire, and even more so when we are young and it is impossible to understand the intricacies of love's delicate boundaries.

\* \* \*

I turned to music. The precious inner perspective that music gives a broken heart can be found nowhere else. With diligence, I practiced, dreaming of stage and recording fame and winning Shelly back. Music was pervasive in my life, relinquishing any chance at acquiring any useful trade, foregoing the procurement of any skill that might make my future more productive. Instead, I concentrated on playing in this band, and the next, and the next. Like true, young suburban musicians, we played music in basements, in garages, on backyard stone patios. Belting out crude renditions of popular music we heard on our local FM radio stations. This was the usual for adolescent just so-so skilled bass players mixing it up with just so-so skilled fellow musicians of the same age, believing music was the way out of small-town New Jersey. Inspired since attending the Woodstock Festival in August of 1969 with Pat and a few other friends, music became the driving force in my life. I saw it originally as a way to reach that star-crested podium and after my first real heartbreak it became the little engine that could win back the heart of the woman I was shedding tears for.

The only other constant in my existence was my friend Pat. We were brothers from different mothers, both musicians, riding the same wave from one group of friends to another, from one group of musicians to another. Pat was the manly, handsome part of our duo, the one the girls noticed first mostly due to how he carried himself. He was born and raised in one of New York City's tougher boroughs resulting in him, at such a young age, having the ability to carry himself with an air of virility and confidence that none of us came close to matching. I lived jealous of him, figuring I was the guy who got the girl that didn't get Pat. He took the brunt of my painful laments of losing Shelly. I'll never know how or why he put up with it for so long, but the worst part is that he eventually became the receiver of the greatest lie I never told.

*Of course you don't know what lie I'm talking about, but I'm getting there.*

It was June, 1971, a month removed from the Kent State shootings, the Altamont free concert in California and its resulting death of Meredith Hunter by the hands of a Hell's Angel ended the 1960's peace and love thing. I was finished with the horror of four years of high school (who let me graduate out of mercy rather than based on my grades), almost a full-year of community college and pop music was becoming the worst trash ever conceived, yet it sold records and made the airwaves.

Enter Bobby James. Bobby worked as an engineer in a studio that Pat and I, through a friend of Pat's, were able to get some work in as studio musicians. A few years removed from sixteen found us capable on our instruments, he on guitar and me on bass. Bobby, who was born an albino, was a keyboard player with a unique voice. His shoulder-length white hair and powerful presence, reminiscent of Johnny and Edgar Winter who were active in the music world then, made him a sure bet to get some decent gigs if we joined up with him, so when he asked us to be in a band, we jumped at the chance. "Great," Bobby said, and got his cousin to play drums.

Playing in a band with Bobby James was largely uneventful except for one fateful night that forever changed my life and initiated the beginnings of the lie that made me an unwilling road warrior. Bobby's father had "connections," and one of these connections owned a night club in Hackensack, New Jersey named The Ironclad. It was rough place to play with a mostly hostile crowd. We were at times scratching our way through requested songs we'd never played before, primarily because they were demanded by some tough characters that we didn't want to have angry at us. Pat and I were playing out for the first time in our lives, and it was a lot more frightening than practicing at the studio. We were both underage, being only eighteen when the drinking age was twenty-one, so we had to apply for a special license to perform in nightclubs and bars, or wherever liquor was present. I was still with Mary, but she was never able to come into the club because of her age. The Ironclad was our home six nights a week, and I was making very good money for a teenager in 1971 but there was one obstacle I had to overcome: the scourge of all young men my age in the early 1970s.

* * *

Shortly after we began playing The Ironclad, I turned nineteen. Too soon after that, I was drafted, having pulled a forty-four in the numbers pool. I was contacted by the local draft board to face the music with the Vietnam War raging. Can you begin to understand the anxiety that can overcome a young man's life when he is called to war and there is no desire to die for country, or at all? Going for your physical after being drafted is a humiliating and humbling process: a long line of young men in nothing but their undershorts parade from room to room, seeing this doctor and that doctor, each one telling you you're fit to serve. Back then, you had to be missing a limb to be 4-F. I vividly recall the hearing test. They placed me in an isolated booth where they put headphones on me and I was told to point to the ear that the generated tone was being sent to. No one failed. If you failed the first time, they kept you there until you got it right. They would have passed Helen Keller even if it took a week.

When it came time for a check of my private parts, the doctor asked me if I did drugs. That was where I saw my opening. I went into the act of a paranoid, delusional schizophrenic, telling the doctor he needed to close the door first because I didn't want to answer with "the man" listening. He had no time for this, which is what I hoped for, and simply said:

"You'll talk to the psychiatrist," before he shuffled me along.

Once with the shrink, I went into a complete shell, swaying uneasily in my chair, fondling the ashtray from his desk, explaining I needed drugs in the morning, in the afternoon, and at night. It was an act deserving of an Oscar, but my real reward was that he deemed me unfit to serve in the US military. At the end of the day, I had to stand before a military tribunal with a member from each branch of the armed forces seated behind a long bench. When my name was called, I stepped forward and was again told I was unfit to serve, and that I could never hold a government or civil job. *Damn*, I thought as I grabbed my voucher for the bus and high-tailed it out of there. I met a buddy from high school at the physical and he didn't do as well. He was assigned a reporting date from the US Army so that night he deliberately sought out a well-known narc in our town and sold him several tabs of LSD. An arrest record involving drugs, especially dealing, was a sure way to avoid Vietnam back then. I was free, (as was my high school chum, I'm sure) to continue living the life of a young, dream-filled aspiring musician from suburbia, New Jersey.

# The Thinking within Me
# Love and Youth

*When young, love is wrapped in a cocoon of physicality, on a par with the emotional attraction that envelops the senses and overwhelms the simple task of everyday living.*

*As with fine wine, love matures with age. It grows in strength with the advent of wisdom and experience. Often such experience can be painful but the heart remembers and builds walls against such onslaughts, should they occur again.*

*This singular, yet complex emotion has been expressed through verse, song, art… every way imaginable. There is nothing that hasn't been written, sung or built in the name of love.*

*Nothing.*

*The words might be different, the melody unique, but they are only an altered perception of what has been done before in the name of love.*

*But what is unique is how each individual feels love **inside**. The internal harboring of such a strong emotion is yours and yours alone, no two are alike. No one can know the depths of your desires, your yearnings, or your perception of being in love.*

*If youth understands this, the journey through life is less distressing when heartbreak introduces herself.*

*Which she inevitably does.*

# Chapter Three
# Hannah

On a warm summer evening in June of 1971, during one of the first nights we performed at The Ironclad, the band was on a break, hanging around by the open club door. The Ironclad was across the street from a drive-in theater, and during our entire tenure there, *Love Story* was the featured movie. We could only *see* the film from where we were, as we were too far to hear any dialogue or music. A blessing, I thought, and later, when I finally did get to both see and hear the film, the blessing was confirmed.

Anyway, a group of girls would often hang out by the club's door to hear the band because, like Mary, they were too young to get in. During our breaks we would perform the ritual of flirting and exchanging innuendos with the girls when, on this one particular night, like Moses parting the waters of the Red Sea, the guys moved to my right and the girls to my left – life was suddenly happening in slow motion – leaving me in the middle and exposing to my direct view the most angelic, sultry, magnificently gorgeous young woman I ever beheld. There stood this absolute vision with long, strawberry blonde hair that framed a face of perfect symmetry with incredibly hypnotic blue eyes, and a strikingly sensuous mouth. To complete a young man's wildest fantasies, she was braless, wearing a thin, white tank top that exposed her generous womanhood for all to see. We looked into each other's eyes only for a few moments, and, like Maria and Tony at the dance in *West Side Story*, the world around us became a vignette, unreal except for the line-of-sight that existed between us in that one instant in time. She was the first to turn her gaze away, never smiling, and the compact world of band mates and girls came back into focus. My friend Pat looked at me and mouthed a silent "*Wow*," telling me that, yes, whatever I was thinking about this beauty, he was thinking, too. But I saw her first, staking my claim with that initial glimpse of her through that sea of youth while her friends flirted and the boys in the band played the man act.

My first thought was that this Venus was out of my league. There was no chance on this earth the most perfect woman I'd ever seen would have anything to do with me. My second thought was Mary, and the third was in complete contrast to the first two thoughts: *I have to get to know this woman.* I must have masterfully flirted because Hannah (yes, this was *the* Hannah) and I ended up in a booth in the diner that was next door to the club talking about the things that teenagers talk about when there is a spark between them. Hannah was seventeen years young, born to Irish and Scottish parents, and lived nearby in Hackensack, and although a natural, native New Jerseyan she acquired the slightest Scottish accent from her father. This was my first moment of being with the woman who would eventually complete the lie that became an indelible part of my life in the years to come; a brief glimpse in time that would be etched into my recollection as one of the most wonderful experiences of my young life. For the second time I actually felt my heart pounding in my chest, but this time it wasn't from the pain of a broken heart but rather from the sheer wonder of Hannah's beauty. Even her scent, that delicious aroma emanating from her, lingered in my senses for as long as I can remember. I wanted time to come to a complete halt, allowing me to sit opposite this princess and get to know everything about her: her likes, her dislikes, her loves, her hates. I was talking too much. *Shut up and listen,* I kept telling myself, but "smitten" is the word most would use here. I fell for Hannah, hardcore, head-over-heels. This moment with her was a dream, but little did I know it was a dream that became a nightmare that I couldn't wake up from no matter how I tried.

Hannah was strong, street tough, and worldly; she got what she wanted. I was putty in her hands, and she knew it. I had never met a woman of such an indomitable and carefree spirit, and found it so easy to embrace. She was a person who didn't care what others thought, finding it important to be herself above all else. Hannah rarely wore shoes, even when she and her friends traveled into New York City to hang out in Washington Square Park. She was shoeless when we met (she borrowed her friend's so she could sit in the diner with me). Hannah loved her family but had taken off several times by her young age of seventeen without any word of where she was going, leaving a desperate and worried father to sit at the kitchen table with an open phone book calling all those he knew to find out if they had seen his daughter. But she always did come back; it was just the space she needed to discover a part of herself that she believed was missing.

The first few nights after we met she came by to spend time with me when the band was on a break between sets. We either grabbed a booth at the diner (when she had shoes on) or just talked outside the club's door, but by the third or fourth night, as we stood by my car in the parking lot I told her that if I didn't kiss her soon I would go out of my mind. Before I could even finish the sentence she took me in her arms and for the first time I tasted the sweetest pair of lips that were even more of a delicacy than I could ever have imagined. With that first kiss between us I was reeling in the euphoric bliss of both romance and lust. Nothing else mattered, nothing else existed, except for her lips on mine, our bodies pressing together as if our very existence depended on it. She could feel I was shaking ever so slightly and laughed at what she assumed was my being nervous not knowing it was anything but. I wanted her so badly that my own body betrayed my then overwhelming but presumptuous desires.

From then on when I was done performing at The Ironclad by three a.m. we stayed together until the sun came up. That gave us about three hours, six nights a week. We spent most of those nights parked in front of her house in my car, passion surfacing at a feverish pace unlike anything I ever knew. Hannah's father worked nights while her mother slept almost comatose, so as long as she was home before her father returned from work, she had the whole night to herself, meaning I had the whole night to be near her. I found it easy to be open and honest with Hannah. God knows why I chose to tell her about Mary, but I did. She accepted it, although she realized that, by seeing me, she was becoming the "other woman", a role Mary once held. This wasn't intentional, or planned, my cheating on Mary, but Hannah overwhelmed my sensibilities. I never thought Mary was someone to discard at my whim but life erects obstacles and I was faced with one. Why I chose not to break it off with Mary to be with Hannah will be explained in due time.

I would leave in the dawn hours, go home to sleep, wake to spend time with Mary, and then return to The Ironclad to begin the cycle all over again. Hannah became my *morning angel* because it was so very difficult to leave her in the mornings when I thought she was at her most beautiful; her flawless features radiated by the dawn's light, but she would always assure me she'd be there the next night when I was done playing.

* * *

There was a problem at home when I was making my living as a musician and keeping these hours with Hannah. It was both a profitable and satisfying livelihood to all but my mother. Mom grew anxious if anyone in the house slept when she was awake, and she had this habit, subtle or not, of assuring that all left dreamland behind when she walked the floors with a heavy step. She thought my sleeping past 7:30 a.m. was out of place, and she would awaken me with the disciplined warning of procuring a 9-5 vocation, or else. I remember being slowly roused from sleep many mornings to find her in my room and well into a conversation with me, obviously begun while I was entrenched in slumber. Since I wasn't even getting home until maybe 7:00 a.m.

at the earliest, this was quickly becoming a dilemma. Frequently, it meant surrendering any chance of staying in my bed, getting dressed and leaving to find sleep at Pat's house.

Finally, to retain my health and sanity, I explained the problem to my father who thought I had a lifetime of work ahead, but, like all of us, just a few short years to pursue my dreams. As such, he felt there was no need for me to dive into the daily grind just yet. He demanded of mother to let me be in the mornings, and she reluctantly acquiesced, though she became convinced my sleeping through the noon hour was not due to hard work but rather to the onset of a "perilous lifestyle" to which my nights were becoming accustomed. That "lifestyle" Mom referred to was a dream-come-true for this young suburbanite; an alluring, seductive goddess from Hackensack, New Jersey.

* * *

Mom did meet Hannah once but only briefly and not under pleasant circumstances. Hannah and a few of her girlfriends decided to take a ride into my town for an afternoon visit on a day when Mary wasn't around. Pat and I hung out with Hannah and her troupe mostly by the high school just shooting the breeze. It was a hot summer day, and Hannah asked if they could come by the house for a drink of water. "No problem," I said, but the problem was that Mom was home and there was Hannah in a tank top with no shoes and no bra, and one of her girlfriends was a black girl from Bogota, New Jersey. Mom was a bit of a racist and was not happy with how Hannah presented herself. She gave me the if-looks-could-kill gaze as we headed down to the cool basement. The girls left maybe an hour later, but my mother made her feelings known to me, expressing her distaste for "young girls like that." I've always wondered how she would have reacted if she knew that young girl she disapproved of was the woman I hoped would become the love of my life?

* * *

Occasionally Hannah and I were able to see each other alone during the day when I was able to get away without Mary suspecting anything. On her eighteenth birthday, I took her to a famous amusement park, its doors long since closed forever. There I was, walking up to her front door and meeting her father, making it our only "official" date. He greeted me warmly, telling us to have a good time in his heavy Scottish accent. Meeting Hannah's father, I began to think this was becoming a serious relationship, slowly escaping the stealth of hushed trysts it had become, through no other reason than my own protective selfishness.

Daytime with Hannah was so very different than being with her in my car at night, or at a friend's house, or – when I could – sneaking her back to my house. In the daytime, walking through the amusement park, she drew the stares, the ogles, of every guy there. I was jealous, protective, but so very meek. Maybe *humbled* is a better description because I carried myself in awe of her beauty. We walked hand-in-hand from ride to ride. She dropped her purse from the top of the roller coaster, and we had to ask the old man who was the ride's operator to please walk in and get it for us. Watching him walking out from under the coaster rails carrying her purse made us laugh, and I'm pretty sure that annoyed him; she was so beautiful when she laughed. We took our pictures in a photo booth, posing cheek-to-cheek. I won a stuffed dog for her at one of the concession stands, and later she tore my shirt, grabbing on to me out of fear when we were in the park's haunted house ride. There was a moment when I teased her about who knows what and she gave me a shot in the front of my shoulder, hitting a nerve and making my arm go numb. That made her laugh again, and seeing her happy was more important to me than a tweaked shoulder muscle.

It was captivating being with Hannah, and often I had to convince myself it wasn't a dream. She would sit up close to me when we drove anywhere, holding my hand or putting her arm around me. I would tell her she was my girl, always would be, and that made her smile. What could this angel see in a skinny nineteen-year-old when she could have had her pick of any man? I asked her once why me, and she simply smiled, telling me I was adorable and that she thought we made a cute couple together. I hoped it was a condition of love being blind. When we were together somewhere alone, I would stare at her, making her at first uncomfortable and then angry, but I couldn't help it. I found her beauty flawless, and gazing at her was a hearty meal for my senses, a delicacy for my very soul. Only a man who truly believes he has found the angel of his dreams can understand what I was feeling then.

There was a place we would escape to on another one of our rare daytime dates way back when; it was a park high above the Hudson River, located on the border of New York and New Jersey. A short distance from the parking lot, we had our own special spot; at a small boulder just off the main trail. It was a place we simply called "the rock". It was low enough and out-of-the-way, a place where we would sit in youthful, passionate embraces and where we would talk of the dreams we had, but I don't recall any of what was said during those conversations. My recollection is that we were together, holding hands over a vista that stretched from the Bear Mountain Bridge in New York, north up the Hudson River, to the George Washington Bridge that lie to the south. We held each other close, standing 500 feet above the river that bore Henry Hudson's name, and at one point while I was fixated on the river disappearing into the horizon Hannah asked me what I was thinking. Nothing, I replied, but the truth was that a moment of reality had set in. I was here with this angel while another thought she had my heart. Eagles, hawks and turkey vultures were our hosts, having nests nearby, and we strolled unnoticed among the bird-watching enthusiasts who came to bear witness to these majestic, winged creatures.

\* \* \*

Mary became aware of Hannah when she showed up one night at The Ironclad to find me outside talking with her and her friends. She had no knowledge of our relationship, though I think, in time, she suspected. Mary took notice of Hannah's beauty. Her jealous and protective nature came through with several comments she made that expressed disdain and mistrust of Hannah. She, more than anyone, knew that my history of being true-blue was tantamount to deception, so who could blame her? Hannah would give me a sideways glance when Mary wasn't looking, letting me know I was a cad, but I think she enjoyed the drama of the moment. It didn't help matters when not once, but twice, at two different parties I accidently called Mary by Hannah's name from across the room. The second time, she was hammered from too much partying. The room went silent – the effect of my social blunder – and Mary unleashed a tirade of names and cursing at me that forced my exiting the party.

I assumed that it was over for Mary and me and raced out of that gathering to find Hannah, who found it amusing when I told her of my gaffe. We spent the rest of the evening together just aimlessly driving around and eventually parking by her house. I felt a release inside, sure that my time with Mary was done and now I could devote all my energy into making Hannah happy. Too soon, I learned it was not to be. Even with my embarrassing her in front of our friends, Mary would not let go of us, despite the evidence on the table. Yes, Mary did stay angry for some time, but she refused to give up on me. For my part, it was turning to resentment that she was hanging on to us. I wanted to devote my life and soul to Hannah. I tried on numerous occasions to make it miserable for Mary to be with me. I did everything short of just telling her about my betrayal, and by this time in our relationship she had to have figured out that I was hiding something, and though I shouldn't have, I stayed with Mary because I was unsure of how Hannah actually felt about me despite the intensity of our moments together. There was passion when we were alone, but we never spoke of our feelings, and too often when we were together her mind seemed to be somewhere else. I sensed she had a reason that prevented her from become completely involved, but my insecurity could not conceive of not having a woman in my life just then, so I played the two hands I was dealt: one during the day, the other at night.

After Shelly, I was convinced that love was over in my life, that never again would I let my heart betray me. Shelly drained every ounce of deep caring I had, or so I thought. In my room one night, Hannah and I were lying in my bed. As she slept, I propped myself up on one elbow to watch her sleep. I felt her breath against my face as I lightly kissed her cheek, and a revelation imploded in my soul: *I was in love with this woman*, deeply in love, hopelessly in love. I recognized the feelings I had for Shelly paled in comparison to how I felt just then. At that moment I knew what it meant to be in love, to care that deeply and honestly for someone. I understood that love was more than just a feeling; it was a longing, a burning inside of you and only the one you love could cool the roaring flames. She was the one I had wished for, and she was my wish come true. I wanted to wake her and tell her of what was in my heart and enveloping my world, but I was afraid she would panic and ask to be taken home. So I gently laid my head on her shoulder, feeling her warm breath against my skin, I pulled her closer to me and fell asleep in her arms; it was the perfect place to be. We slept till just before dawn. When I drove her home I planned to let her know how I felt before she got out of my car.

But I never told her. Not then, not ever. Her eyes were always watching the horizon when we were together, even in our most tender moments, and I wanted her to be *with* me, totally in spirit as well as body, when I found the words I needed to say. I never found that moment, and there were words I lived to regret never saying. Inside I cursed Shelly for this failure to tell Hannah the desires in my soul, for causing my emotions to create walls, barriers against releasing the deepest expressions in my heart for fear of being hurt again. Following that night, each time Hannah and I were together, I searched inside for the strength to let her know of my heart's desire, but I was such a damn coward and so very afraid of what I would hear - or might not hear - back from Hannah. I realized how would she possibly believe me if she knew I was still with Mary? I could have, should have, broken it off with Mary by now but all I could ever think of was the pain I felt when Shelly left, how Mary was there with me through all of that, and there was just no way I wanted to put her through that heartbreak. I did try - believe me - but empathy or maybe just faint-of-heart surfaced each time.

* * *

Near the end of the summer, 1971, Pat decided he had enough of the band and left to explore other avenues. I stayed on with Bobby James for another few weeks until I too felt the urge to try something else. This created an entirely new quandary with my seeing Hannah. Without the six-nights a week band gig, I was relegated to seeing her late in the evening after dropping Mary off at home. Fortunately that scenario was short-lived because Mary started working in a new job during the day and since I was unemployed the situation reversed itself and my days were devoted to Hannah. But as fate would have it, what was so perfect a life I felt I was living became a harbinger of disappointment and heartbreak.

I drove a 1963 Ford Galaxie 500; in fact, my first three cars were all '63 Ford Galaxie 500's and all of them were mechanical nightmares. Driving down Route 17 south in New Jersey, somewhere around Rochelle Park, mid-October, 1971, my car gave up the ghost. A gas station manager was kind enough to let me park it behind his shop until I could make arrangements to have it moved. He told me the motor had seized and I should have been watching the oil. When I asked what it would take to fix it, he laughed and said, "This baby ain't going nowhere anytime soon." My thumb was now my mode of transportation - a foreshadowing of my future - and a genuine grease ball picked me up in a customized 1965 Mustang. Guess he wanted to impress me, but hitting over 100 miles an hour on Route 17 was terrifying, and I lied that the next exit was mine. Walking the rest of the way home was exhilarating because I was still alive.

Only now I had no vehicle, and I was supposed to pick up Hannah who, unfortunately, lived some distance away. The worst call of my young life came next as I phoned her to let her know I no longer had a car, no prospects for a car, and therefore no way to see her until I could afford a new ride and I had no way of knowing when that would be. There was a momentary silence, then Hannah told me that if *she* really wanted to see someone, not having a car wouldn't stop her. She'd hitchhike to where they lived. I took that to mean that "if" was only *if*, and she had no plans to stick her thumb out to be by my side. Thinking back, it serves to reason that maybe she meant quite the opposite; that if *I* wanted to see her, I would hitch the ride there to be with her. Maybe that's what she meant. With a lump in my throat and using all the strength I could muster inside to not have her hear the quivering in my voice, I said goodbye to my morning angel and hung up the phone. It was all too easy and over so quick, it seemed unreal but solidified my belief that to Hannah I was just a guy she spent time with. I was nothing special to her. For that moment in time I was torn: should I call her back? If I wait a few minutes more, will she call me? The world, my life, was eerily quiet except for my thoughts.

I assumed that would be the last time I ever spoke to Hannah. I never thought I could feel worse pain that I had when Shelly told me good-bye, but I was so very wrong. I stood leaning against the desk in my room. "Birds" by Neil Young from his *After the Gold Rush* album was playing on the record player, Neil was singing "*It's over*" and it seemed as if he was singing those two words to me at that painful moment in time. Now my world was no longer quiet, my heart was pounding loudly, desperately trying to beat its way out of my chest. Though I didn't completely breakdown as I had with Shelly, the subdued but painful interlude that followed was a far more powerful, more personal heartbreak. I stood quietly with tears streaming down my face for what seemed a very long time. I wanted to scream, maybe scream for help, scream for Hannah, but instead I chose to simply stand there and let life kick me in the nuts. Why couldn't I get Hannah to fall in love with me? What else could I have done? Questions that plagued my soul for years to come.

Now, some will ask: how could I have fallen so deeply in love with Hannah? They will ask that when they discover I was only with her for five months. Not enough time to get to know someone, and especially not enough time to fall in love, they will say. But love doesn't recognize time; it just is when it is. Love doesn't have a schedule. It shows up when you least expect it, and can disappear in an instant, taking all you have, leaving you empty and broken. It's been said that "love begins with a smile, grows with a kiss, and ends with a teardrop." Losing my Hannah was akin to losing my very soul, my reason to exist and I think that had I been a lesser man...

# Chapter Four
# The Lie is Born

What was I to do? I was so alone, and there was no one to speak to, no friend who would tolerate me acting like a fool again over another woman, especially after only a five-month relationship. I was certain to be scorned, considered weak. Imagine trying to explain my hurting so deeply over Hannah when the company I kept knew I was still with Mary, and these same friends put up with my lamenting over Shelly more than they should have. I am not a man who contains grief very well - at least I wasn't then- so I decided on a course of action that would forever be a falsehood in the most ludicrous fashion imaginable. Hannah completely cured me of Shelly, made me realize how what I felt for her was only puppy love and losing her was like a child losing a favorite toy, unaware there are so many other toys in the world. Of course, the world didn't know my revelation; the world didn't have to know that, so I chose to grieve over Hannah *but use Shelly's name whenever my grief surfaced.* After all, I was still with Mary, the only two friends who knew of Hannah were Pat and Mike - and to them, she was only a fling I was having on the side. If a conversation came up about girls, and especially if I was high, I was prone to outward displays of mourning lost love, but I never deviated from my substituting Shelly for Hannah. *Pride goeth before a fall.*

I didn't write to Hannah as I did Shelly after our breakup, but when I had a vehicle, even sometimes using Mary's car, I would drive past her house, sometimes park nearby, hoping to catch her outside. I never had the courage to just go up and ring the bell. I found out later that she ended up singing in the band with Bobby James, even living with him for a while, and that was a stab in the heart. I saw her again only in my dreams and in my memory.

Every day.
Every night.
Week after week,
Month after month,
Year after year.

I remained with Mary only a month after Hannah. I unfairly blamed her for my loss because I suspected that Hannah's reluctance to love me was partially because I stayed with Mary during our time together. I never told her how I tried on so many occasions to break it off and I suspected she wouldn't have believed me anyway. What woman would? One day, a day too late for Hannah and me, that all ended. On that day, as I sat by my desk and Mary lay on my bed, the words poured from me, surfacing from some place deep inside, unfurling like a banshee from my thoughts, and it was as though I was hovering overhead watching my body telling Mary there was nothing there for me any longer. She completely lost it, and that was a very rough time for both of us. From my room, we ended up sitting at my parents' kitchen table, with Mary crying uncontrollably. Once again, Mom was nearby, but the roles were reversed: I wasn't the one devastated. My mother's first thought was that Mary was pregnant but when I told her that wasn't it, she quickly realized what was happening and left us to ourselves. She really liked Mary and was sad to know we were at the end of the road. Like everyone else in my life, I never told her about Hannah and if I had, she would have been angry with me. I regret now hurting

Mary, and I wish I had known another way to handle that situation. I'm sure there was but at nineteen I couldn't come up with one. Mary deserved better - and, as it turned out, she got it in a few short years when she met and married a good man who gave her a good life.

## The Years behind Me
**1972**

- *Five White House operatives are arrested for burglarizing the offices of the Democratic National Committee. This is the start of the Watergate Scandal*

- *The book, "Joy of Sex" is published. Spends more than 70 weeks in the top five bestsellers list*

- *Ray Tomlinson invents email*

- *"American Pie" by Don McLean is released*

- *Last U.S. ground troops are withdrawn from Vietnam*

**1974**

- *Richard Nixon resigns as president of the United States following the Watergate Scandal*

- *World population is estimated at four billion*

- *"The Exorcist" is released in movie theaters*

- *Elton John's album, "Goodbye Yellow Brick Road" hits the U.S. charts*

- *President Ford announces an amnesty program for Vietnam War deserters and draft evaders*

**1975**

- *The Vietnam War ends as Communist forces take Saigon and South Vietnam surrenders unconditionally*

- *Patti Hearst Becomes Most Wanted and is Arrested for armed robbery*

- *"Love Will Keep Us Together" by Captain and Tennille is top selling single of the year*

- *Muhammad Ali beats Joe Fraser in the "Thriller in Manilla" match*

# Chapter Five
## At the Crossroads

After Hannah, life went on; a life that I knew wouldn't include my morning angel. But what choice did I have? I started yet another band with Pat and a few other local musicians. This is where I met Jayson who was to become one of my dearest friends. He moved from Vermont to New Jersey in early 1972 with the intention of playing in the band as our keyboardist. We were writing and performing all original material: high-energy instrumentals that were some of the greatest pieces I ever had the privilege of performing in. Sadly, the band didn't work out, but Jayson and I had a strong chemistry right from the start. He became a shaggy-haired, bespectacled creative force in my life, becoming part of the group that knew of my lamenting over Shelly, and in the course of a few social gatherings was where he learned about her. Naturally, Jayson assumed my heartache was due to her loss. He had no knowledge of Hannah, she remained my secret, and I feared how weak I would look to this new friend if he became aware of my pathetic emotional disguise. As I grew closer to Jayson and got to know him I discovered I was jealous, or envious, of the family he came from. They were some of the most amazing people I ever had the pleasure of knowing. Jayson's dad, Joseph, was an art professor and a great photographer and when I became entrenched with the love of photography, Joseph gave me so many useful tips; tips that proved their value when I chose to pursue a short-lived wedding photography career a few years later. He was also an amazing artist, his oil-on-canvas abstract paintings were textual beauties; but Joseph never enjoyed sharing them with anyone except with his wife Rose. Their love was one of legend and from first meeting them anyone could see, despite all their years together, they still shared the excitement of being in love that must have been there from their very first time together. I envied what they had and hoped someday others could levy the same claim about me and whoever would become my lifelong companion. I hoped then, as before and for some time to come that person would be Hannah.

\* \* \*

As is the normal course in the life of a socially active nineteen-year-old, my circle of friends expanded and a new group of local girls began to hang around our inner circle. One of them was a tall, attractive brunette named Carrie-ann. Again the competition began among the males in our tribe to vie for her attention and whatever else we could get. A year later in September, 1972 I married Carrie-ann (who was *not* Irish). Just as I was unfair to Mary, I was even more so to this woman who loved me and whom I professed to love, despite knowing where the loyalties of my heart really belonged. She easily assimilated into my group of friends who at some point and for whatever reason made Carrie-ann aware of my grief over Shelly, particularly when I was prone to demanding isolation or remained aloof and distant at moments when it was a distraction to what was occurring around me. I am also certain there was a point where I let my guard down and in a drunken stupor rambled on about the agony of lost love and cursing Shelly's name in the presence of my friends that included Carrie-ann. She was completely unaware of Hannah's existence, and if she believed I was elsewhere when we were physically together because of Shelly it was better that way. At least for me.

One incident in particular stands out during our brief marriage: My parents were away on vacation, and Carrie-ann and I promised to stop by the house daily to tend to their dog. We took turns, alternating afternoons and evenings. One afternoon after I let the dog out into the yard, I sat by the dining room table and, as was usual in moments of quiet solitude, thoughts of Hannah came streaming into my consciousness. I found a small 3x5 notepad on the table and proceeded to write her a note I knew she would never see because I would never send it to her. I told her how much I missed her and how life was just too hard now, but after writing it, I immediately tore it up and threw it away. In the evening when Carrie-ann stopped by to let the dog out and sat at the same chair in the dining room, she noticed the imprinted words that appeared on the blank sheet that was underneath the one I wrote on. Being a smoker, and having a lit cigarette with her, she dropped ashes on the paper and lightly rubbed them in, bringing into full view my betrayal of our marital bond. But the impression of Hannah's name was not legible so she assumed it was a note to Shelly. She raced home in a tearful rage and that evening a screaming, hurt, and angry Carrie-ann was destroying our apartment before finally locking herself in our bedroom, asking me through her tears, "How could you?" There was nothing I could do, and telling her the note was not intended for Shelly was the last thing this woman needed to hear or would accept. I simply left and moved temporarily into my parents' basement. Believe it or not, our marriage didn't end there. Carrie-ann called me in a few days and told me she forgave me and understood I had a problem and wanted to help me get through it. The sad part was she had no idea what my problem was, only the lie that I let her and everyone else believe. What a scumbag I was!

But my problem doomed our marriage from the very beginning; she just didn't know it. Staying with Carrie-ann was not going to work for me. I was not in love with her, and I wanted to just move on. One month shy of our second anniversary, I broke her heart by telling her I was moving to California with Jayson and Mike. She and I had been separated for a short time when I told her this, but she always thought there was a future for us. Carrie-ann begged me to come home, and a back-and-forth ensued with me giving reason after reason why that wasn't going to happen, until she asked me the inevitable, "Do you still love me?"

"No, I'm sorry. No, I don't."

That I was paraphrasing the words I heard from Shelly years ago didn't escape me. Somewhere inside I cringed at the possibility that I was executing payback; payback for the hurt and the pain caused by Shelly, or by Hannah. Carrie-ann didn't deserve this; she loved me, was devoted to me. How I despised that part of me that even considered that a moment of revenge. I left a crying Carrie-ann alone in the last apartment we shared together. Again, I just set myself up for some intense karmic penalties I'm sure were coming my way.

If there was a purpose of having Carrie-ann in my life, I think it might have been for expanding my musical curriculum. She gave me my very first flute as a gift one Christmas, it was an instrument I expressed my love for and had a strong desire to learn to play. I taught myself the basics and eventually was able to study under a few excellent teachers. The flute would become a dominant part of my life, allowing me to express in music what I never could playing the bass. Its sound and the emotion I attempted to display with each and every note became my "religion," the closest I believed I would ever get to an after-life Utopia if one did exist.

\* \* \*

Jayson put the idea of California on the table. It was already in my plans to get away, move out of New Jersey, and try moving forward elsewhere I just didn't know where. Jayson's girlfriend, Susan, had moved to Oakland recently and expected Jayson to join her. He told me of his plans to do exactly that, and the timing couldn't have been better since I was separated from Carrie-ann and knew staying in New Jersey was the last thing I wanted to do. I told Jayson to count me in and we could drive out via my van. Mike liked the idea of change himself and said there was one last truck delivery to Ohio he needed to make for some extra cash. We planned on spending a week or two in Vermont with Jayson's folks before heading west. Mike's plan was to make the Ohio trek and then take a bus to Bennington, Vermont, where we would pick him up. He said his delivery to Ohio and back shouldn't take more than a day or two.

The night before our leaving, friends helped us pack up my Dodge van by Jayson's house. It was a 1970 Dodge A100 that Mike customized inside with bunk beds where the top bunk folded down to form a couch. It also had shag carpeting, a cork ceiling to improve the sound of the 5-speaker 8-track player, custom lighting lining the inside roof, a side window with a screen and translucent casement vents with an inside crank to open or close them, and a roof vent. The outside was kept barren, needing a paint job. We wanted to avoid any attention on the road and thought it wise to keep it original. From the mid-1960s on through the early to mid-1970s, vans became a target for law enforcement to pull over without just cause. It was an early case of profiling, particularly those vans that were emblazoned with contemporary pop-art or peace symbols, with beads for curtains and bumper stickers denigrating Nixon or Vietnam. Jayson and I didn't need to become a target, so my beautifully designed interior of my Dodge van was masked by a shell needing body work and a paint job.

I was financing my trip, along with the expenses accrued through the overhaul of the inside of my van and its motor, by selling bags of "double crosses," a popular amphetamine of the day similar to "white crosses," only twice as strong (hence their name.) I kept lots of several thousand in my cardboard dresser, one hundred to a plastic bag, in my cellar bedroom in my parents' house, and the dresser was located right next to the back door! Anyone could have discovered my stash simply by opening the middle drawer; they weren't covered very well. It was a case of hiding in plain sight. It's too easy to say now, in retrospect, I am not proud of this method I chose to finance my journey, but those were different times with a different atmosphere. Doing what I did would not be acceptable at any time under any conditions but the drug culture among the young back then was not being offset with the overwhelming media and legal edification of the dangers of street drugs. The mindset of the 1960's, embellished by movies and rock music, carried over into the early 1970's; marijuana was on a par with heroin in the eyes of the law. We got high by any means possible and I saw it as an opportunity to profit from that mentality.

On August 9th, 1974, Richard Nixon had just resigned as president of the United States. I watched his resignation speech at the house of my first flute teacher, Leigh. He was a brilliant musician that I wish I'd have had more time to learn from, but we were leaving the next morning so I said my goodbyes and headed to Jayson's. At midnight when the job of packing up the van was done and everyone went home, I drove by Hannah's one more time. I didn't park but drove slowly in one direction, turned around, and rode past her house again. The pain in my heart and soul was almost too much. I felt foolish to still be in love with a woman I knew only for a short time, and now I was a stalker! The drive home found me angry with myself. I knew it was time to move on. It was now three years later, and it didn't make any sense to feel this way.

So, the next day, Jayson and I left on the first leg of our journey: to his folks' house in Arlington, Vermont. This new beginning would surely push Hannah out of my mind. I have the fondest memories of the previous summer I stayed at Jayson's parent's Vermont home when I was separated from Carrie-ann. It was so easy to feel alive and unburdened there, amidst the beauty of the Vermont countryside, free from the weight of my New Jersey lifestyle. Their little home in Arlington, a former hunting lodge over a hundred years old, was to be our launching area for the trip west and where we would wait for Mike ... only, Mike never made it. On the quick delivery side-job he took, he got careless and swallowed too many pills to stay awake, but that wasn't what they did for him. Instead, his body said no more, no matter what, and it rebelled, putting him into an unrecoverable stupor. The police report said he fell asleep at the wheel of his truck just before it veered off the highway and tumbled down an eighty-five-foot embankment off of a highway in Pennsylvania. His poor head slammed unmercifully off the truck's cabin windows and walls. Mike hated to sleep, but swallowing more and more pills to stay awake caused a mutiny inside his tall, skinny frame, and this mutinous consequence put him into a sleep from which he never recovered.

It was Mike we called when we had car trouble, or needed a few dollars, or a place to stay, or just needed a friend. Our tall, unwaveringly devoted Greek friend never turned his back on a call for help. How dare we look at him as an equal! Regardless, we did, and not until many years later did I realize we were small packages among his bounty of worldly goods. Like me, Mike was born and lived his younger years in Passaic, New Jersey, but unlike me, Mike carried over the wisdom and survival instincts of growing up in that tough city. Raised by a single mom with a younger brother, he was the first friend I knew who had to fend for himself from morning to night until his mother finished her workday. His self-awareness and confidence was years ahead of his age and his self-taught mechanical skills impressed even those much older mechanics who did consider him an equal, despite his youth.

After the accident Mike was moved from Pennsylvania to a hospital in Dover, New Jersey. I would call the hospital room every day before we left and would speak to his mother, asking how Mike was doing. His mom was always optimistic, as a good mom should be, I guess. At some point we got the devastating news that it was unlikely Mike would ever recover, and I cried when it all set in, breaking down in the kitchen of Jayson's parents' home. His mom, Rose, was with me, and the comfort I received from her helped me get through that dark moment. It was news I had to accept, but I wondered about Mike's mom. How could any mother ever accept such news?

During this time of waiting for news about Mike, I had the opportunity to jam with several of Jayson's musician friends. They were all jazz buffs, and though I wasn't at their level of musicianship, I was able to hold my own. We'd jam in Jayson's parents' house, in an old barn of one of his friend's; outside in another friend's backyard...some of the best memories of performing music occurred while I was there in Vermont. Any opportunity to play, especially when life was throwing curve balls, was a welcome retreat. Throughout my younger years it seemed music was always there to soothe the savage beast I called existing.

When the dust cleared from the disconsolation of Mike's accident, it was time to make a decision. Jayson and I chose to leave because we knew staying would have accomplished nothing, and it wouldn't have helped Mike in any way whatsoever. Jayson's girlfriend and a new life were waiting for him in California, and I was running from so many things; so maybe we were motivated by selfish reasons to move on. I used the rationale that, if it were me, I would have wanted Mike to get on with his life, but maybe that was no more than poor solace on my part to satisfy my conscience.

# The Thinking within Me
# What is a Lie?

*We all know what a lie is. We have all heard them and have been liars ourselves. Often it isn't with malicious intent but it happens.*

*The dictionary defines a lie as an "untruth, or falsehood" or "something intended or serving to convey a false impression". That last one applies to my story about Hannah.*

*In retrospect - and hindsight is ALWAYS 20-20 - my falsehood wasn't necessary. There was no reason to live so many years deceiving so many people and when I discovered that it was a fabrication created by my own self-preservation I had to admit it was unnecessary to construct at all.*

*But sometimes a lie can act as a shield against a painful truth, or allows us to keep our pride in certain situations. These untruths can carry the weight of years and none would be the wiser unless the liar comes forth and puts all the cards on the table.*

*And afterwards, a liar revealed holds a lower status among friends, family, etc. Aesop wrote: "you cannot believe a liar, even when he is telling the truth". Therein lies the problem: backed into a corner with a deception you've worn on your sleeve for so many years, it takes a strong person to come forth with the truth.*

*I was not a strong person.*

# Chapter Six
# The Road ahead of Me

Late in the summer of 1974, Jayson and I said goodbye to his folks and drove north through Vermont, trekked across Canada by way of the Kings Highway, and came back south into the States via North Dakota. At the Canadian-North Dakota border, a border guard made us unpack the roof carrier on my van that held everything we owned. It took over an hour to get everything down since most of what we owned in the world was on the roof of my van, boxed, tied and packed and the intention was not to unload until we got to our destination. After the work was done, this bastard opened one bag, took a peek inside, and then said, "Okay, you can put everything back."

My sometimes youthful, rebellious, James Dean-like attitude quickly surfaced. I retaliated, against Jayson's urgency to let it go: "Are you kidding?" I said angrily. "That's all you're going to do is peak in one bag after all that work?" I was steaming with anger, overflowing with a careless, tumultuous sense of reprisal, my voice elevating in pitch and a sense of vengeance seeped into my thoughts. But the border guard was oblivious to my rants, ignoring me like I was yesterday's news while he used a magnifying glass to search the shag rug of our van inch by inch for marijuana seeds, but to no avail. I will tell you that it was Jayson's foresight to stop somewhere and vacuum the hell out of the van while I saw no purpose in being so diligent. I could feel

Jayson grabbing a hold of me, whispering into my ear and reminding me that we were carrying a substantial amount of pot and getting this man angry could lead to much greater consequences. After his scan of my van's floor, he just smirked and walked back into the small office trailer where he hung his hat and ate his donuts. What a fuck-face! We were carrying weed, but our hiding spot was so clever and indiscreet that it would have taken a better border guard than this guy to find it. As we were repacking the roof of my van I was caustic in my outloud comments that as I think back, was so foolish.

The weed we had so cleverly concealed was weed we picked up in Thunder Bay, Canada, when we approached a long-hair on the city street and asked him where we could "cop some pot." He directed us to a pool hall on the next block, gave us a name to ask for (which I can't recall), and off we went. The person we sought out was a tall, shady character with a mullet, wearing sunglasses on an expression-less, mustached face. His wide-collared paisley shirt was opened at the top by four or five buttons, exposing his black chest hair, supporting a bevy of gaudy medallions on chains. He gave us the once-over and then brought us to one of the billiard tables. The top of the table was hinged on one side, and as he lifted it up, we saw an amazing volume of bags of marijuana inside. He told us to pick out what we wanted, and we did. I was so uneasy as we exchanged our money for his pot because it seemed the entire place was filled with hoodlums more than happy to take back the weed and the rest of our money. We left as quickly as we could, grateful to just get out of there with a few ounces of pot and our lives!

After leaving the Canadian border we drove west to the coast of Washington, where we made a left and headed south to the promised land of California. All in all, it was an eventful three-week road trip that brought us to the west coast, living along the way out of my van, parking for a night's sleep in open fields, deserted strip mines, beneath the Space Needle in Seattle; just to name a few locations. We found refuge on the floor of a friend's apartment in Portland, Oregon for a few days. One time we even tried parking the van in a beach parking lot along the Oregon coast, only to be woken up by a park ranger and told we can't sleep overnight in a state park in Oregon. We weren't even aware it was a state park, but in any case, we drove aimlessly for the next few hours until we found a small dirt road that led to nowhere. It was better than nothing, so we parked the van and got a few hours of sleep. We ate when we could, mostly just one meal a day that Jayson would put together using our small propane burner stove. He would prepare our dinners catering to my vegetarian diet, even though he himself wasn't a vegetarian. The man tolerated soy meatballs, soy chicken and whatever else I was accustomed to simply because he was a friend above and beyond what that title meant.

Jayson was a great road companion and the decision to travel with him to California had been an easy one to make. He was a talented piano player, artist, and photographer, and I learned so much while in his company. When we would come upon a small town on our journey, and particularly if it was near the end of a day, we'd look for a local tavern or restaurant: someplace that might have a piano. If it did we'd ask for the manager's permission to perform for the evening crowd and often they didn't mind. We'd play a few mellow pieces with Jayson amazing the local folk with his keyboard ability while I was slightly more than passable on my flute, particularly to any non-musicians. Made a few bucks here and there through tips but it wasn't so much for the money that we played as it was for the love of music. My most vivid recall of our impromptu performing was at a small local waterhole in Shelby, Montana. The folks there were so genuinely appreciative of two young men on the road performing for tips here and there to get by. Though we played mainly jazz which wasn't exactly the music they were familiar with, they were generous with their tips and applause.

\* \* \*

The journey was an adventure in spite of the overshadowing sadness of having a friend on death's door and my unrelenting longing for Hannah. It was a trek one could be grateful to have taken when so young, just for the memory of it. I took along a bagful of change, using payphones when I could find one to call the hospital room where Mike was being kept. His mother stayed by his side and sounded happy to hear my voice. I called just about every other day, but couldn't help but wonder if she felt some bitterness that I chose to leave in spite of Mike's condition. Years later, I discovered that she was angry and hurt at my deserting her son's side.

* * *

By now, I was aware it made little sense to disguise the truth about Hannah, but sometimes one can become so ingrained in a deception that there is no way out. When Jayson asked me why I was moving to California, I would tell him it was about needing change, escaping a bad marriage, seeking a more rewarding life, but the truth was that I desperately needed to put some distance between my memories in New Jersey and a new life someplace else. It was foolish of me to not realize that, no matter how far and wide one travels, your memories are always right there, the painful ones in the forefront of your mind, pounding on your temple from the inside. There was some consolation in the fact that Jayson never met Hannah but he was aware of Shelly and unfortunately he bore witness too often to my being drunk or high and becoming despondent over lost love. I was so skilled now at maintaining the lie of Shelly for Hannah that even when I couldn't see straight I held my guard in that respect and Hannah's name never rolled off my tongue. So for our trek out west I kept the secret of my heart hidden from Jayson believing that was one less diversion we didn't need between us.

But there was a moment where my fortitude almost lapsed and I came ever so close to telling him everything. We were driving through Glacier National Park in Montana, desperately in need of a bath or shower and we couldn't find a campground that would let us, even for a fee, use their facilities unless we stayed for the night; and that, we weren't prepared to do. Most campgrounds would allow us, for a minimal charge, to replenish our water supply and use their shower facilities, but not here in Montana. On Highway 2 East, a road that cuts through this magnificent, beautiful part of these United States, we came across a waterfall called the "Silver Staircase Falls." It was a natural step formation carved into the side of a granite mountain by water, easily scalable, so we decided to climb up as high as possible and bathe where we felt safe that no one could distinguish what we were doing. It was an arduous climb, and once we found a plateau that was reasonably wide and we could wash in safety and out-of-sight, we settled in to wash up. What we didn't expect was that the water was so cold it was nearly unbearable. Putting our heads in the falling water to wash our hair could be done only in spurts of seconds because it was a painful task. It seems the water was a runoff from one of Glacier Park's remaining glaciers – melting snow, in other words – and it was by far the coldest water I ever used to wash up with.

When we were done and ready to head back down, we took a moment to marvel at the vista bestowed upon us from our lofty heights. It was a long way down to the van, and across the road there was a quick-moving stream that was located at the base of an even taller mountain than the one we were on. Halfway up that mountain, there were railroad tracks, and a very long freight train was cutting its way along the mountain's face. The scale was so incredibly grand that my perception became distorted, and what I was looking at could easily be discerned, in my mind anyway, as a model railroad display constructed by a very ambitious hobbyist. It was one of the most striking panoramas I've seen in my lifetime, and, as always, I thought of Hannah and wished she was sharing that moment with me. I turned my gaze to Jayson, who was admiring the same view, and I thought the timing was right to tell him about Hannah, to let him know this unforgiving memory inside that wouldn't let go. Before I said anything, I turned back to the opulence enveloping our world and decided, no, it wasn't the right time. That moment was meant only to stand in awe at the creation before us. Jayson and I climbed back down, refreshed and ready for the remainder of our journey to the west coast.

* * *

Our three weeks on the road ended for Jayson in Oakland, California, where he moved in with Susan who was already settled in a decent apartment. I stayed only three or four days, using some of that time to take the BART into San Francisco to visit my sister Peggy. It had been years since I last saw her. She lived with Travis in a magnificent apartment at the crest of Scott Street on the top floor of a building with a sunroom that overlooked the entire city. Travis was a black man Peggy met while living in New York City, but they moved to San Francisco years earlier to avoid the scrutiny and interrogation she knew she would have gotten from our family had they stayed together living back east. She said my father was not happy with her decision, and Peggy reiterated a comment he made as to her choice in men. For all his faults, I never found Dad to be a racist or even the least bit discriminatory toward people of color or different nationalities. He never seemed to mind my black or Hispanic friends, but maybe when it came to his oldest daughter, it was a different story. Something must have transpired that sparked Travis's hatred of our family, and it seems that extended to me; he was not very happy that I was visiting or going to spend the night. Travis ranted loudly how Peggy's family doesn't care about her, how her father was useless. It was as though he didn't see me in the room, or more likely he didn't care. He was both tall and muscular, very menacing looking. Uncomfortable and uneasy both explain how I felt at that moment, meeting Travis for the first time. Peggy assured me it was okay, and she told me the couch in the sunroom was my bed for the night.

In the silence of that evening, basking in the tranquil glow of the lights of San Francisco, my thoughts turned once again to Hannah. Travis' reaction to my visit and Peggy's comment about how Dad reacted badly over her choice of this man made me realize it was the same response Mom had upon meeting Hannah, even if it was only briefly. At this point in my life I knew very little about Peggy – she moved here to San Francisco when I was much younger - but it didn't escape me being aware of the bond we shared over loving someone that our family rejected.

Over the city, the full moon was rising. I had developed a ritual of speaking in low tones to that glowing orb on the chance that Hannah was looking up at the night sky when I was and she would hear, or sense, my words. When love, or rather the absence of love, causes pain you can physically feel in your heart, anything, any action that might bring even a glimmer of hope … you take that action. From Peggy's apartment, there was a vista of San Francisco that included the Coit Tower atop Telegraph Hill to Fisherman's Wharf. It was easy to speak to my night sky guardian from that room, easy to hope, but too easy to feel the heartache I carried.

The following morning, after spending some time with Peggy, catching up on all the latest family news, I returned to Oakland for what amounted to a short goodbye with Jayson. I headed south to Anaheim, land of Disney, where I stayed a few weeks with my cousin Lenny, who was older than me and living the straight and narrow lifestyle with a wife and daughter. While staying with Lenny I was able to find work at a local drugstore as a stock clerk. Soon after that I found a studio apartment in an old, rundown dive called the Lincoln Motel, one block from Knott's Berry Farm. They gave me the keys to a studio apartment towards the back on the second level. The place had a rancid smell with a bed and couch that looked like they were purchased at a fire sale. When I opened my kitchen cabinets for the first time, I disturbed a very large family of cockroaches, causing them to scurry in all directions, but I only vamoosed in one: to the main office. They apologized and explained there were no other rooms available but if I wanted to come back later they would have the room fumigated. There was no choice for me, really. I couldn't afford anyplace else, and living with my cousin was pleasant enough but restricting so I replied I would be back later.

When I returned, the cockroaches were all gone but the smell of the fumigation was overwhelming. I opened the windows, and rather than drive back to my cousin's, I slept that night in my van in the motel's parking lot. By the following afternoon, I was settled in my new furnished apartment, needing only to bring in the few items I owned in the world. The place had a queen-sized bed located directly beneath a large picture window that looked out over the motel's parking lot, which sat above one of the tributaries of the Los Angeles River. Beyond that was a vacant lot, overgrown and strewn with junk. The couch next to the door was older than me, and only the powers that be knew what tiny creatures lived in its interior. The kitchenette had a small sink, refrigerator, and electric stove. My only skillet was a camping pan with a foldaway handle that I used to cook all my food, including toasting bread.

During the second night and my first sleeping in my new apartment, I was awoken by the sound of my door opening. When I turned on the light, I saw a family of four standing near my bed that included a very young boy and girl. Since I was wearing only undershorts, their mother quickly rushed them out of the room. They appeared to be Polish, and the father's accent confirmed it when, after I determined it wasn't a dream, I asked what the hell they were doing there. He explained the front desk said my room was available and gave him the keys. It was around 12:30 a.m., and I assured him it wasn't available. They left, and somehow I fell back to sleep. The next morning, I went to the front desk to inquire what was going on. The clerk and the manager apologized profusely and said someone had mistakenly written down that I didn't take the room after the cockroach incident. Honestly, though, I thought they were just fucking with me and getting off on it. I probably thought that because it seemed whatever pair were working the front desk always appeared to be in the throes of having had too much alcohol.

\* \* \*

An earthquake was the event of the evening during my third night at the Lincoln. Like most people, I had never experienced an earthquake before, and it is not something to add to one's bucket list. I woke to my world – my entire world – shaking, while a low, deep rumbling reverberated in the background. The picture window next to my bed was buckling, waving in and out. I jumped to my feet when I realized what was happening and gathered myself to bolt for the door, but as quickly as it happened; it was over in an instant. Turning on my bedside radio seemed the logical step, and I learned that the Los Angeles area had just experienced an earthquake of a medium magnitude. I couldn't sleep the rest of the night. The next day at the drugstore I could only marvel at the nonchalance my coworkers expressed over the previous night's earth-shaking event. The following two nights brought small aftershocks; quick, short, earth-shaking events to add to my frightening experience.

The Lincoln Motel was Anaheim's equivalent of a slum, but it was the best I could do. Besides, it provided me with the solitude I sought except for the all-too-frequent police raids of this unit or that unit. In fact, they became so commonplace that I slept through most of them and would discover what happened the next morning from one of my nomadic neighbors.

For the most part, I kept to myself in the beginning. Not knowing anyone equates to a party of one, and that made it easy for me to drown in my sorrows. Self-pity is one of the easiest emotions to express. I was a paradox: lonely but wanting to be left alone. Almost every night for months, I sat in the dark in my seedy room facing the big picture window and staring out into nothing beyond my own self-introspection. When the moon was full, I had a friend to talk to. I used the cigarette I was almost done with to light the next one, and I clung to the bottle of Jack Daniels I drank to exaggerate my misery.

At times, I even found myself believing in a higher deity, or just hoping for one. If there truly was a God, I begged Him for the salvation of my soul as I felt my heart trying to tear itself from my body. Tears would come and go; nights would come and go. I spent my days working at the drugstore, where the owner despised (I could never figure out why) but tolerated me because I was a hard worker and kept to myself. The job paid so little that I would steal small packets of

Oreo cookies when I was very hungry; my principal diet consisted of stolen cookies and Carnation evaporated milk. I spent Thanksgiving alone, turning down my cousin's invitation with the excuse I had to work. Christmas Eve turned out to be a twelve-hour work day, and afterwards I was invited to the home of a new friend I met at work to spend the holiday with him and his family. I accepted the invitation, but I was so exhausted that, within the hour, I fell asleep on a chair in their living room. They let me be, and when I awoke all the other guests were gone. I apologized for being a poor guest and went back to the apartment.

On Christmas Day, I did spend a few hours at Lenny's house with his family. New Year's Eve, I accepted another invitation to a party and wound up completely and utterly rip-roaring drunk. I woke up on the floor of a bedroom with a girl that I worked with at the drugstore in my arms and no memory whatsoever of what happened. She remained aloof and embarrassed after that and would never give me the details of our encounter. New Year's Day it was 80 degrees, and I took a walk wearing shorts and a tee-shirt, thinking what a difference if I was back home where it was probably below freezing and how uncomfortable I would be, complaining about the cold. But I wouldn't be alone. My walk took me miles away to nowhere and even resulted in my becoming lost. I eventually found my way back. I was no longer alone in California with new friends but it didn't stop me from feeling destitute and the invasive pain that loneliness can cause. Finding my way back to my room still found me lost when the door closed behind me.

\* \* \*

It was hard to believe that not that long ago I was lying in my sleeping bag on a large, flat rock that jutted out into Harriman Reservoir in Vermont, watching a rare but barely visible display of the Aurora Borealis that flowed under the backdrop of an incredibly clear night sky that Vermonters are accustomed to. Only a week prior to that a few of us had hiked out to that rock at the end of the day and wound up having to spend a cold night through no choice of our own. Harriman Reservoir is a beautiful, pristine body of water off of Vermont's Route 9, and we couldn't resist its beauty. We were just out for a drive to explore the countryside when we pulled into the reservoir's parking lot and found a trail that looked to be a good hike for the five of us: me, Jayson, Susan, Jeff (Jayson's friend), and Mike. The trail was narrow and winding with parts of it as much as ten feet above the water. It brought us to the flat rock that, at its widest, was maybe fifteen feet out from the shore. There were two rocks actually, side-by-side, and on the other rock were two young ladies who had set up camp for the night with a tent and a good campfire going. They invited us to hang with them, which we did. Of course, getting stoned was mandatory. After a few hours, we laughed our way into forgetting that we should have left for the van before it got dark. With a sense of panic, we attempted to hike the trail back, but it was pitch black. Once the trail entered the overgrowth and trees, we realized it would be far too dangerous to attempt the hike. We weren't equipped with flashlights, all we were wearing were shorts and tee-shirts, and it was beginning to get chilly. The five of us returned humbled to the girls' campsite, where we pleaded, asking if they would mind if we just sat around the fire till morning. These girls were good people, and not only did they insist, but they provided each of us with either a blanket or a sweatshirt. It turned out to be a memorable evening that passed too quickly; before I knew it, daylight was moving in.

As fate would have it, and she often does, one of the girls had a grand opening of a coffee house she put together later that day in the nearby town of Brattleboro. She was able to rent a large floor above a row of stores on the main drag, but she had no entertainment scheduled. Jayson, Jeff (who was an outstanding drummer), and I offered our services to come and perform for her opening night. The room had an old upright piano for Jayson, and it was located in the center of the room atop a small, wooden platform maybe fifteen feet by fifteen feet that served as the stage. We improvised the entire evening, mostly on classic jazz numbers, and the high ceiling along with the room's natural reverberation allowed me to project the sound of my flute effortlessly on all registers. It was one of my favorite nights of performing and one that I will always cherish. I wish we'd kept in touch with those girls. I do remember that one was named Emily, and she worked at a motel called the Marlboro Inn on Route 9 near Brattleboro, but the name of the girl who ran the coffee house I can't recall. Wherever they are, I speak for all of us when I say: "Thank you". One week later, we were back at the rock in Harriman, this time equipped with flashlights and sleeping bags, but the girls weren't there. That night, after we crawled into our sleeping bags, the "Dawn of the North," or the Northern Lights, loomed overhead, and I wanted to believe this heavenly display was an omen that was assuring me that my life ahead would be prosperous and overflowing with hope and fulfilled dreams. If wishes were horses, and all that but I wished Hannah was there with me, thought of how proud she might have been had she heard me playing in Brattleboro, especially since I considered her my muse with every note I produced.

But that was then and I wasn't in Vermont anymore. I was back in my dingy dwelling in the Lincoln Motel in Anaheim, sitting on an old, broken couch thinking of Hannah and how ashamed she might be to see me now in the state I was in. Regardless, I ached for her so. A man alone crying over lost love is not a man who admits as such. Why couldn't I find the strength to move on? Why was Hannah so embedded in my heart, my very soul? This cruel God knew why and if He was there He wasn't answering. I've spent my life angry at a God I'm not certain even exists, and losing Hannah at an early age was the onset of my Agnostic rebellion.

# Chapter Seven
# Mail Call

In California, mail was an elixir. It became easy to understand the value of mail from home for those who are living distantly, whether by choice or otherwise. I heard from my parents, my brother, cousins, friends: half of whom begged me to come home, while the other half wrote about how they were thinking of moving to California themselves and would I be able to put them up for a bit? I never responded to those letters. I wrote to Shelly just to say hello and to tell her of my new life. I also wrote to Hannah, but the tone of that letter was so different. It was clear and to the point: telling her that I missed her, and would she consider giving California a chance? In the letter I told her that I had a place for her to stay and that I was working and how different life was here. Only Shelly wrote back, several times: I never heard from Hannah. It was safe to assume my morning angel had all but forgotten me and that writing back wasn't worth the effort. For all I knew, she could have still been with Bobby James. I considered writing to her again, but no reply to a second letter would have been more than I could have handled.

I heard from Pat a lot. He missed me, as I did him, and he was so talented and creative that I always anticipated his letters with excitement. They were filled with cartoon drawings of me or other friends, and memorable moments of our lives together, and I would laugh out loud at his inventive communiqué. After a few letter exchanges, I decided to tell Pat about Hannah and how I used Shelly as a cover-up for a broken heart. It was a long-winded letter, several pages in length that I decided to mail the next day. That following morning, I read what I wrote and elected against telling Pat the truth, or the lie I was living. It was an easy decision because I relied so much on what he thought of me; I didn't want to take any chance of jeopardizing that. I did write him another letter, telling him I still carried the hurt of "Shelly" and I had hopes California would help me to overcome this personal torment. He wrote back that I wasn't in love with Shelly: he said I was in love with the *ghost* of Shelly and that I needed to realize that so I could get on with my life. I knew his words were an attempt to have me see things more clearly, or at least the way he saw them. In reality, Pat believed I couldn't get past Shelly and there was such a guilty feeling on my part, misleading a good friend who stuck by me when I wore my heart on my sleeve, but what was done was done, and I never approached the topic of Shelly in a letter with him again.

My brother Bruce wrote me, too. He was back east in jail, but I can't remember why he was put there. Letters from him came fairly regularly, and I found them the saddest because I knew he had a good soul and a good heart and that he was where he was because he was a follower, easily susceptible to those who misled him. It was this weakness that incarcerated him and sadly, it was his innate ability to follow and not lead that resulted in his premature death years later at the hands of a sixteen-year-old drug dealer with a gun. Most would assume it naturally that I would tell you how amazing a man he was, despite his run-ins with the law from time to time, and predictably most would then assume that was only my point of view and that, of course, being blood, I would come to his defense. Understood; but no one I ever knew that met Bruce didn't take a liking to him immediately. He was eleven years older than me, short in stature but big in heart and soul, quiet, and unassuming. He was always in great shape and carried himself proudly. There was nothing he wouldn't do for me and I for him.

My father wasn't Bruce's natural father, and sadly Dad had no use for him. His real father was a man my mother hooked up with while he was passing through town on his motorcycle (circa 1940). Mom married another man (not my father) after Bruce's father took off, to give Bruce a last name. It wasn't until I was in my teens that I learned his surname wasn't even his birth surname. Bruce finally met his real father who lived in Florida just a few years before his natural dad passed, and he also discovered he had another brother. Bruce was raised by my mother, my maternal grandmother, and my aunt with my Dad merely living in the same house. With no strong male influence, I believe this caused Bruce to kowtow to the wrong type of men simply because they took command. Some of his friends frightened me, and I could never understand why he chose them as companions. One in particular made Charlie Manson from 1969 seem like a choir boy: he was so demonic.

After serving his time, Bruce straightened up his act and married a good woman named Rosalie who gave him three beautiful children. Bruce was a player, and it was rough for Rosalie to stay with him, but when she died well before her time, Bruce realized what he lost. He moved to Ohio to be near his daughter and grandchildren, but he lasted only a few more years before his life was cut short before his time.

Writing letters, sometimes to no one except myself, helped me pass the time, and it was a place to dispel my grief without any visible displays from me. I was trying to develop a style of prose and poetry that had an identity and was unique only to me, but most of what I produced was trash except maybe for a few pieces. My words were written on the pages of a small, homemade, felt-covered, blank-paged book that Jayson made for me before we left Vermont. It was now filled with random nonsense, but to me they were insights into a soul I was trying to recognize. My favorite was a short, rhyming poem I composed while one night sitting in the open doorway of my van's side doors in the Lincoln Motel parking lot. It was a brisk, somewhat clear Californian evening, and looking up at the few visible stars, I was inspired by the passion of my own depression:

*I come from the stars, am part of the sky,*
*my life is a demon that does nothing but cry.*
*Grasping each morning I call to the past, confused*
*towards my bad luck that love didn't last.*
*"I want nothing! Need no one" save*
*my angel's call. But I come from the stars …*
*and it's such a long, long way to fall.*

Hannah needed glasses to see clearly, especially at night, but her vanity wouldn't allow her to wear them and she didn't like contacts. I knew of the glasses but never saw her with them on. We were sitting in a park one evening, and she looked up and commented how the street lamp above us looked like the moon. It was so quiet, so still, with the warm summer air embracing us. "That IS the moon, Hannah," I replied, realizing then how bad her vision really was. I noticed how her hair glistened in the moonlight; how I could almost see a halo around this angel. She was from the heavens, not from New Jersey, not from this mortal plain. That night in the park I told her that I was from the stars, a messenger sent here to bring her back with me, away from all of this. It was the closest I ever got to telling her how deeply in love with her I was.

"You're crazy" she said, "but sweet", then she kissed me lightly on my cheek.

I wrote those seven lines that captured perfectly both that evening with Hannah and the streetlamp and the grief of the memory it inspired within as I sat in my van beneath southern Californian skies. Seven lines that displayed how deeply a man's soul can descend into pain and loneliness. It was with that poem at that moment that I believed my voice was becoming unique and even if the poem seemed juvenile to some, I didn't care. I understood my destiny, though it wouldn't be fulfilled for many years to come.

\* \* \*

Eventually most of the people I had heard from back east stopped writing. Though solitude was my chosen path for the first several months, we are, after all, social creatures, so I began to consort with the local indigenous folks. I made several new acquaintances, mostly guys who played guitar or piano so we could gig as a duet: me on flute and them on whatever. We would play coffee house gigs because they were in vogue in Southern California and there was practically one on every block. You could just walk right in, and if there wasn't already entertainment, a simple introduction was all that was necessary because you were performing for no more than tips. There were two fellow musicians in particular, both guitar players that I gigged quite a bit with. It was an easy way to make small change. I always performed with the passion available to me at that moment, and with each job we could get, I would try to display the ardor that enveloped me the night I played with Jayson and Jeff at the Brattleboro coffee house, but I never was able to recapture the inner glow of that evening. Each coffee house looked just like the last one; the indifferent clientele that sat there were basically immune to our presence, jabbering away about their redundant, claptrap lives. Sometimes I would get so angry at their apathy toward our performance I would blow out a hard high-register C note on my flute that would stop a room cold with the shrill piercing that resonated from my instrument. The people there always became angry, always looked annoyed, and needless to say they weren't generous with their remunerations after we were done performing. My partner would be annoyed at me too, but I didn't care. There was a malevolence inside that matched the pain of lost love, and music was both the great soothsayer to calm me and the catalyst to arouse the bile of my demons.

I remember one night in particular when me and a guitar player performed at a coffee house, scheduled to play after a quartet of young men, all on guitar, had just closed their set with a song entitled "Fuck that Girl." Actually, I'm only guessing that was the name of the tune because it seemed to be the only words in the song. The reserved, hippie, up-and-coming yuppie crowd was stunned but got off on the balls these guys had. It was a tough act to follow. Needless to say there was no need for a piercing high-C that night to draw the crowd's attention.

# Chapter Eight
# Busted!

The door to my studio apartment at the Lincoln was set back off of a second story walkway. Making a left toward my door, there was a wall containing a picture window belonging to another apartment. Two girls moved into that apartment shortly after I moved into mine. They were neighborly and very friendly, but they were the principals in a terrifying memory of my time in California.

Their picture window had a sliding glass pane with a screen. One afternoon, I was sitting in the open window just shooting the breeze with one of the girls when her roommate came walking in. She had just returned from the mall, and following behind her was a stocky man with a thick mustache. He was wearing a straw hat, Hawaiian button shirt and sunglasses. The girl I was talking to asked her roommate who the guy was. The roommate replied she had no idea, seeming surprised to find the man there, when suddenly he pulled out a gun with one hand and a badge with the other. He screamed:

"I'm a cop! Nobody move! Nobody fucking move!"

I could feel the blood rushing out of my face when another plain-clothed officer from seemingly out of nowhere grabbed me and told me to crawl through the window into the girls' apartment and lay face-down on the floor. The place, within seconds, was swarming with cops. I was told again not to move, not to even lift my head off the floor, and

I did what I was told. They meant business and still had their guns out. Meanwhile, I had no idea what was happening or why, and I had to lie in that prone position for two, maybe three hours. During that time, it was obvious what I had gotten into: the girls were heroin dealers and had been the subject of an investigation for some time. When it came time for the detectives to address me, one of the girls did come to my defense, explaining I was only a neighbor and not part of their dealings, nor was I a user. The cop who grabbed me brought me to my apartment and said I would need to show him some ID.

We walked into my place, and there on the bed was a bag of weed and a pipe, and I resigned myself to my fate. I told him I had no defense or excuse for what he was looking at, but to my surprise the detective took a look at my driver's license and said they didn't have time for the small stuff. He told me to just put it away and to stay in the apartment until the scene was cleared. My heart was still racing when I finally left my place and everyone was gone.

A few days later, I saw one the girls in their apartment gathering her things. She told me she was out on bail but had to find somewhere else to live. I asked about her roommate, and I discovered that after she walked in the door and realized the guy following her was a cop, she bolted into the bathroom and swallowed *nineteen* small balloons filled with heroin. She ended up in the hospital where they pumped her stomach and kept her on an IV to clean out her system. I never saw or heard from them after that. I have no idea what happened to their lives, but they were certainly two people I will never forget. Their apartment remained empty for the remaining duration of my stay at the Lincoln Motel and for a while it was back to being quiet. Too quiet, really. Despite new friends and coworkers the noiseless solitude of my evenings pulled me into a funk once again but this time I was determined to keep my head above the fray.

\* \* \*

When living the life of a recluse came to a close, I even tried dating again; thinking maybe putting myself out there would help me get on with the task of living. In the same mall as the drugstore where I worked, there was a diner where I would often take my lunch break; usually not able to afford anything more than a cup of coffee and maybe a bagel. I became friendly with a cute waitress named Elaine, who had short blonde hair, hazel eyes, and a look that went from serious to perky so easily. She would bring me a bagel, or even a sandwich, and she made sure it was "on the house" from time to time. On October 30th, 1974 – an easy date to remember because Muhammad Ali had just beaten George Foreman in Zaire to reclaim the heavyweight boxing title – I mustered the courage to call the diner and asked her out on a date.

She seemed happy that I called, and the next night I picked her up at her house. What we did or where we went escapes me now, but after spending some time together, I discovered she was only sixteen. Since I was twenty-two, I quickly saw a formula for trouble I didn't need, but still I hung around longer than I should have. Elaine lived with a very dysfunctional family in rather squalid conditions. Her parents had to be aware that I was much older than their daughter, but it didn't faze them. They were very pleasant and amicable toward me, but somehow their casualness didn't sit right. One afternoon Elaine paid me a visit to my room with her five-year-old brother in tow and proceeded to try and get intimate with me on the bed. That was when I knew she was living the life of a sixteen-year-old, thinking like a sixteen-year-old, dismissive of any consequences from her actions, and that was also the last time we were together. My only attempt at romance in California was a disaster and the only benefit, if there was one, was that it helped me out of the shell I was living in.

Unfortunately, the downside of my now-active social life was an increase in my drinking and drugs which until that time I restrained myself from indulging to any excess. Getting high or wasted only magnified my miserable existence, but I yielded just the same. I attended a party at an apartment of someone who lived in my complex, got rip-roaring drunk, and left to stagger back to my room. On the way I needed to gather my clothes from the laundry room where I put a load into a dryer a few hours earlier only to discover they had been stolen. In the haze of my recall, I did see a young lady rushing from the laundry room with a handful of clothes before I entered but thought nothing of it. When the realization hit me that all the clothes I owned in the world now was what I was wearing, I returned to the party and made a complete ass of myself, bawling like a baby, making everyone uncomfortable. Needless to say, no one from that gathering had any interest in becoming or remaining my friend. If there is a good side to this story, it came from the women I worked with at the drugstore. When they learned of my plight, they all brought in second-hand clothes from their husbands or boyfriends for me to keep. One doesn't forget such kindness.

Despite my occasional social ineptitude, my excessive drinking and drug use became an escape from life's bullshit, and this all led to meeting my soon-to-be roommate, Ray. He was a friend of one of the musicians I played with, and he worked as a maintenance man in the motel where I lived. Ray and I gradually became buddies because of an incident where he actually saved me from a small, angered mob that dragged me out of my motel room and proceeded to pummel me until Ray stepped in. I was returning one night from working late at the drugstore, parked in the lot and cut through the laundry room into the courtyard where my room was located above. I could hear some kind of ruckus going on and as I walked through the court yard and up the steps to the second floor landing where I lived, I noticed people quickly closing their doors when they saw me. Didn't give it too much thought, entered my motel room and closed the door behind me. Within minutes there was a pounding on my door, an angry pounding by many hands. I opened to find out what was going on when a small group of people grabbed me, pulled me out into the landing and started yelling at me: "where's the gun", they shouted, "where's the motherfucking gun?". These screams were followed by punches being thrown at me, took one to the side of my head, my chest, another made my legs buckle and I almost fell to my knees. It was a frightening ordeal and all I could think of was to fight back. I had no intention of going down without a fight. That was when Ray came into my life: he pushed through the small mob and got himself between me and them, screaming "this guy's cool. I know him" when in truth I wasn't sure if we'd ever met. The crowd backed off as Ray assured them I wasn't the man they were looking for. Seems moments before I got home some lunatic was running through the motel yard shooting off a gun. I didn't see anyone when I arrived home but apparently I just missed him, walking into the courtyard moments after he ran out. Those people who saw him leave where I came in assumed I was the one with the gun but Ray assured them I wasn't and that seemed to be enough so they backed off. No apologies, nothing, just an angry mob dispersing and leaving me to lick my wounds. Ray helped me into my apartment and I couldn't thank him enough. Who knows what would have happened to me if he hadn't been there?

I discovered Ray knew me through the social contact of partying with common friends, says we met at the home of a friend we had in common. I had no memory of meeting Ray prior to that night but then again, I couldn't even recall the party he was referring to. He was one of my new breed of comrades: those I got high with. Ray even got me a job as his assistant maintenance man at the motel when I lost the gig I had at the drugstore. Ray was truly nomadic, living with this friend, then with that friend. The most recent friend warned me that having Ray move in with me could be bad news, but I turned a deaf ear to this advice. Ray was born with the smarts and an amazing aptitude for all things mechanical, and in this respect he was so much like Mike that I couldn't help but be drawn to him. As it turned out, Ray's former roommate was right: Ray was a parasite, and though the signs were there, I couldn't recognize or refused to acknowledge them. He lived like a slob and helped himself to anything of mine he desired. I would come home from work to find an apartment full of people partying and eating every last bit of food and drink we had. Still, I tolerated him - even though I now understood the warning I was given about

Ray - because I had become accustomed to company. Maybe I simply thought he would do until something better came along.

His one endearing grace was that he owned a motorcycle and taught me to ride. I was enthralled by the freedom that being on a bike presented, and I sold my Dodge van, the last remnant I had of Mike's handiwork, so I could purchase my own motorcycle. It was a 1970 British Triumph 500 import with the gas and clutch on opposite handlebars from an American bike. After some trial and error and failing my road test at the California DMV, Ray and I took rides every day, traveling miles up and down the California coast. I found it so thrilling, such a release from the bullshit of life, that one day together we decided that a road trip was calling to us – southern California was nowhere – and Alaska lodged into our psyche as a great destination. So that was where we would be heading.

My last night in Anaheim, Ray and I decided to have a big blow-out party at the studio apartment we now shared, inviting the people we had befriended over the past year. It was a great turnout with so much weed being passed around I imagined I was in a club in Amsterdam, getting high without abandon or fear of recrimination. I recall the final discussion that circled the room: If a man falls from a plane and you hit him with your car before he hits the ground, essentially making that the cause of his death, would that be considered mercy killing?

Absurd? Yes, but it got the room roaring with laughter until the knock on my apartment door. Amidst the festive atmosphere, I opened the door and was greeted by the sight of the Anaheim Riot Squad, in full gear with helmets, shields, and night sticks. My heart seemed to stop, and I could feel the blood rushing to my face. Everyone in the room reacted the same way, but a few gathered their wits quickly and most of the marijuana found its way to my sink's garbage disposal. There was one uniformed officer not in gear, standing to the side, and one of the ready-for-combat gendarmes spoke:

"We've received a report of a marijuana party going on in this apartment."

I asked, "Do you have a warrant?" with a courage, or maybe anger, I pulled from somewhere inside. The officer not in gear responded:

"We don't need a warrant for a situation like this. Would you ask for a warrant if we heard a gunshot inside?" I was as confused as everyone else who heard this absurd statement, but I was getting angry, too. I said:

"Well, you didn't hear a gunshot inside, and I'm not letting you in."

The officer turned to one of the battle-geared cops and asked, "What would be the proper course of action now?"

The cop replied, "There's nothing we can do. We should move on."

The uniformed cop agreed and just like that, they were gone. By all appearances, this was a practice run for a squad of rookies. When my blood pressure finally returned to normal after they left, it appeared all of our "friends" had conveniently left too without saying a word, and I never even noticed them slipping out. That was the last night Ray or I ever saw or spoke to any of those folks, and they probably all breathed a sigh of relief over that fact anyway. Besides, we knew it was our last night, so we just cleaned up and prepared for the next morning. Ray did comment how impressed they all were when I put on my lawyer suit as the shit hit the fan and wouldn't back down from our unwanted visitors. I wore a badge of honor that night; fervently defending what I thought was a violation of my civil rights, that no one or no organization should have the wherewithal to abuse. Of course, the hypocrisy doesn't escape me: we were smoking dope, a highly illegal thing to do in 1975.

The next morning, sometime around the middle of July, 1975, we hit the road on our machines - me with nothing more than a rider's permit - and drove out of Anaheim with an eager anxiety of what the future held. The first item on our road agenda was to stop by my cousin Lenny's house, both to say goodbye and to thank him for everything. It was a rather sad parting, and it was also the last time I ever saw Lenny.

\* \* \*

Ray and I drove northwest on through Los Angeles via Route 5, picking up Ventura Highway (the song of the same name by America began playing on a loop in my head) and staying on that beautiful road until we connected with Route 1. There is something surreal about riding on a motorcycle on the open road; the only sounds you hear are the noise from your bike and the wind hitting the sunglasses on your face. But the loudest sounds are your thoughts. Again, I thought of Hannah and what the projections of my life ahead could possibly hold for me. Where was I going to end up? Would it be Alaska? If so, would she be so enticed, so tempted out of curiosity to join me there? How easy it would be for me to just grab the next highway back east and in a few days knock on her door, if only to see her briefly. She didn't hate me when we parted, did she? Or was I still the man who would ride past her house, or park nearby to watch for her, never once having the courage to walk up the steps and ring her doorbell. "Hello, sir," I would say to her father. "I was wondering if Hannah might be home today?" Would it be different this time? What made me think I would act any different after driving 2,850 miles to her neighborhood?

On the road, Ray and I lived on coffee, slept beneath a canopy stretched over the two bikes parked close together, and enjoyed the camaraderie of other riders we met on the road. It was all a real adventure ... until we reached Big Sur. Big Sur is a sparsely populated region of the central coast of California where the Santa Lucia Mountains rise up from the Pacific Ocean. The name *Big Sur* comes from the Spanish name of that area, *el sur grande*, meaning "the big south," referring to its location south of the Monterey Peninsula. During a run on Route 1 through this magnificent region, Ray's motorcycle ran out of gas. We had no idea where we were or how far it was to the next gas station, so we hung for a bit on the side of the road and decided to light up a joint while we figured out what the best plan of action should be – not too wise a move under any circumstance.

Getting high was our first mistake. The second was when we tied a rope from my bike to Ray's and decided I would pull him up the highway. Route 1 in Big Sur is a winding, one lane road, and as I rounded the first curve, Ray lost sight of me and panicked. He hit his brakes, and I was thrown back and to the right, my bike tumbling alongside me. Ray followed moments later, rolling through the gravel into the same clearing and it was only the grace of a higher power that there was a clearing there at all. The other side of the highway was a drop of several hundred feet into the Pacific Ocean. I wasn't badly injured and was able to quickly get to my feet. I ran to find Ray in the swirling dust, almost bowled over by his speeding past me to turn off my bike which was still running and could have exploded in a gaseous ball had he not had the foresight to save the day. That would have been a hard lesson learned.

Needless to say, we were pretty banged up with bruises and scrapes on our arms and legs, but it could have been much worse. A van full of guys passing by stopped to help us, picking up our bikes and asking us if we wanted to be driven to a hospital. They did what they could, and though we and our bikes were in bad shape, we decided we could fend for ourselves. We were to spend nearly a week in Big Sur buying bandages and ointments and other meds, licking our wounds while Ray did the repairs on our motorcycles.

That first night following our accident, we slept on a hillside high over the ocean. Lying there in our sleeping bags, wincing from the scrapes and burns, we were being entertained by the heavens themselves, watching shooting star after shooting star blaze across a night sky so thick with starlight that it was as if we were chosen exclusively to enjoy the product of the universe's proudest achievement. With each blaze of light trailing across the billions of shimmering pinpoints overhead I reflected on my life and how I got to this point. Fully aware that I was still so young I knew that there were demons I had to wrestle with, to overcome so that I could cease to dwell on what was and what might have been.

The next morning as we were packing up to head down to the highway, a herd of cattle came down the mountain trail. At their forefront was a large bull, and when the herd stopped upon seeing us, the bull feigned charging several times. We moved slowly, not sure what to do. If he charged, we were fucked, no question about it. After a few anxious moments, a couple of men – herders, I guessed – came down the trail and steered the animals around us. It was yet another notch in our survival belt that we would rather not have had.

While we were in Big Sur, we made friends with another biker, Bob. He was a nice enough guy who was riding alone from and to destinations unknown. He seemed to me almost too much of a straight arrow to spend time on the road alone, traveling from somewhere to nowhere, but I was too inexperienced to judge anyone's character and besides, it wasn't any of my business. The three of us had dinner the first night we met Bob in a roadside restaurant built in all pine with pine-top tables and chairs. I sat at the head of a long table with Ray and Bob on either side of me, and three young ladies sat at the table to my left. The girl at the table's head wouldn't stop staring at me, and though I was aware of her gaze, I never acknowledged or responded to it. She was gorgeous: long, brunette hair with hazel eyes (guess I did peek, at least once) with a face that could turn heads, except she didn't turn mine. The accident we had and the drugs we took to recover wiped me out, and I just sat there numb. Ray and Bob kept pleading with me to react and start up a conversation, but I couldn't get myself to do it. Our meal ended, and we left. My two companions were not very happy with me, but I didn't care, not then.

The following day we took a ride to Pfeiffer Beach; a beautiful and secluded park near Big Sur with amazing boulder formations that line the shore. One large boulder framed a huge hole carved right through its center by the onslaught of the ocean's waves over many thousands of years. We also discovered areas where the sand was purple, and we later learned this was from manganese garnet in the hills being washed down the creek to the beach. Another marvel of nature that she shared with me on this journey.

It was a great afternoon where we just hung out, smoked pot, and laughed away the hours. In the parking lot a short distance from the beach, we met a few guys who were also partying, and they invited us to join them, which we were all too willing to accept. Just a ways down in the same lot, I noticed the three girls from the restaurant who were getting into their car to leave. Thanks to the weed, I felt none of the inhibitions that engulfed me the night before at the restaurant, so I strode over and asked them if they would like to stay a bit and party with us. The girl with the gaze directed at me the night before wanted to stay and tried to persuade her friends to do the same, but it didn't work. The other two didn't like the looks of our newly-acquired friends and had no interest in socializing, so off they went. I never found out that stunner's name, but I figure, if it was in the cards, it would have happened. I don't know why, but she stays in my memory as another "what if." Too bad but, with so many things in life, probably just as well.

After nearly a week, our time in Big Sur had come to a close. Our wounds were healed enough to ride, and thanks to Ray our bikes, for the most part, were roadworthy again. We knew that Alaska was no longer an option. Our funds were low, and my motorcycle, despite Ray's mechanical prowess, was acting strangely. I called Jayson in Oakland, who now had his brother Devon living with him and Susan. I told him of our accident and Big Sur experience and asked if we could come north and hang there for a bit while we figured out what we were going to do. Of course, he said it was okay; I never doubted it would be otherwise, so we said goodbye to Bob and set off north to Oakland.

\* \* \*

Staying "for a bit" at Jayson's place turned into a two or three weeks crash. I discovered Jayson had another roommate named Barney; a tall and lanky fellow with long brown hair with an equally lengthy beard. He never wore shoes, but his personality was so vibrant you couldn't help but want to get to know him better. It seemed that, no matter where Barney went, he was well known and well liked. I remember attending a party in San Francisco, a high-end yuppie gathering, and Barney in his unkempt shoeless persona seemed so out-of-place, yet he was greeted so warmly and affectionately by everyone upon our arrival. He was a genuinely decent fellow. I learned that a short time after we left Jayson's place, Barney passed away, the victim of a hit-and-run driver while he was crossing the street near his house. The good die young I've been told...such a loss for this world and a gain for the next.

As I did a year earlier, I took the BART again into San Francisco to visit Peggy. She was no longer living in that magnificent apartment at the crest of Scott Street; instead, she and Travis had moved to a small, dark basement dwelling. I didn't understand why they would have gone from where they were to here, and I don't recall asking. I'm sure they had their reasons. I also don't think I stayed too long with this visit. Peggy had somewhere to go, clad in business attire, but she did tell me Travis was playing with an African music ensemble in Berkeley and I should check it out. I told her I would and said goodbye to my sister, whom I wouldn't see again for another several years.

It was an easy enough commute from where Peggy lived to the University of California, Berkeley where Travis's band was performing outdoors on the college's main lawn. He played an African percussion instrument, and quite well, too. The music was eclectic and tribal with roots deep in the culture of African rhythms. When the band took a break, I walked over to say hello to Travis. I didn't know what to expect, remembering how the first time we met he resented my being in his apartment, but at this meeting in Berkeley, he was exasperated, totally taken by surprise at my visit. And he was cordial, not angry or contentious – to say he was overly friendly is putting it mildly – he wouldn't look directly at me, instead he directed his focus elsewhere as we spoke. I could tell he wanted it to be brief, so I excused myself and said, "Well, it was nice to see you again, but I guess I should leave. I need to get back."

"Sure, man," he said, shaking my hand. "You take care."

I left. Later, I learned that he was cheating on my sister, and his girlfriend was with him at the concert. He was worried that she would join us and he'd have to figure out how to introduce me. Pretty funny, when I think back on this, even Peggy gets a laugh out of it. She later told me Travis never mentioned my visit but she did catch him with this other woman not too long after his performance in Berkeley. They separated shortly after I left.

During this stay in Oakland with Jayson and Susan, I received a call from my father back east that Mike had passed away. His passing wasn't unexpected, but I, like anyone would, always held on to the hope of a miracle. He never came out of his coma. Both my parents – and particularly my dad – took his death very hard because they grew to love Mike. The bond had developed during the time when Mike lived with me at their house for the few months before we left, Mike to Ohio and me to Vermont. My father asked me to come home on that phone call, and with that, our destination was clear. Ray and I had nowhere else to go, really, and we couldn't stay with Jayson indefinitely, though I suspect he wouldn't have minded if we tried. So, Ray agreed New Jersey was in our future.

My father wired us $50 (back then, if you can believe it, that was more than enough for gas), and again I found myself saying goodbye to Jayson, the man I journeyed here to California with a little more than a year earlier. That moment and the memory of it come back to me with mixed emotions. I am certain if Ray wasn't with me, I would have stayed with Jayson and tried to make a go of it, but life is somewhat planned beyond our control, and even the parasites like Ray can serve a purpose. However, the reluctance on my part to leave my friend's home in Oakland was overwhelming at times; I was so afraid of what was waiting for me in New Jersey. A year away wasn't nearly enough time to camouflage the pain I still held inside. There was a moment during my stay that Jayson asked me if I would try to contact Shelly when I got back. I wasn't sure if he noticed the embarrassed, almost shameful, look on my face, but in my mind the defenses I developed came in to play and Hannah became Shelly.

"No," I told him. "I know Shelly's moved on, and I have to do the same." It was strange to hear myself saying that four years after that last phone call to Hannah. God, how I wanted Jayson to know the truth, but I was locked so solidly into this falsehood it became a part of me, and I figured it wasn't hurting anyone. After all, why would Jayson care who it was who damaged me? It might as well have been Shelly for all he knew. The ridiculousness of the situation did not escape me.

# The Thinking within Me
# Memories

*I've come to learn that memories, especially distant ones, are not reliable. We apply an emotion to a memory that is often different than what it was the moment the event occurred. That is understandable; time has a way of distorting reality when it comes to momentous events in our lives.*

*But not the memories of the heart. You can't remember loving someone if you never did. The heart is more reliable when it comes to recalling an emotional attachment, whether of love or hate, that existed somewhere in the past.*

*It is amazing the level of recall the mind can bring forth when piecing together events from previous days, months, or even years. The exact details of each occurrence might be shrouded in detail, or altered in perception because the emotional memory is not the passion that was prevalent at that point in time.*

*This is where the heart comes in. Its emotional memory is flawless, unnerved by the onslaught of subsequent events, or the passing of time.*

*The array of circumstances might not be completely accurate, but only in detail would they be in error as long as the heart found its place among your words.*

# Chapter Nine
# The Road Back Home

*The shadows are all heavy now,*
*everyone's run to hide. It is so*
*lonely to be alone ...*
*or am I scared to die?*

It was sometime around mid-August when Ray and I left Jayson and Susan's house in Oakland, headed east on Route 80, which actually travels northeast for a good distance until it levels off and beelines across the USA straight toward the George Washington Bridge in New York. The ride back east with Ray was uneventful early on, until we hit the desert in Nevada. Twenty-six miles from the nearest town of Battle Mountain, my bike began to smoke, then hemmed and hawed and finally stopped running. We were literally in the middle of nowhere, my motorcycle was dead, and it was beginning to get dark. While Mike was being mourned in a closed casket somewhere in New Jersey, I was stranded in a desert in Nevada with a broken bike. *Mike could have fixed this*, I thought, but Ray couldn't.

As the sun was setting, he worked feverishly on my problem; meanwhile, we were getting eaten alive by all kinds of insects. A trucker driving a flat-bed stopped and offered to put the bikes on his empty trailer and drive us as far east as he could, but it was obvious to us he was drinking so we politely declined. We made a desperate decision to get off the road and stay the night in our sleeping bags, determining it best to try again in the morning. We pushed my bike off the highway onto a dirt road that seemed to end in the shadows of small buildings that we could barely make out in the dark. Once we stopped where we felt safe, we crawled into our sleeping bags. It was sweltering and barely breathable in our nylon cocoons, but we dared not come out of cover as we could hear the hordes of insects striking the outside of our bags. Though I didn't think it would be possible, I did eventually fall asleep. This was the first of two times I had to force sleep on this journey to avoid dealing with extreme conditions.

In the morning, we were woken by the voice of an elderly woman who was standing over us, asking, "What in the world are you doing here?"

When we were able to sit up and focus on our surroundings, we noticed the structures we saw only as shadows in the dark were various sized sheds arranged side-by-side in two opposite rows as if they were their own small town. We explained our situation, and I guess she took pity, inviting us into her "home" for breakfast and coffee. We thought it strange that she opened the door to one of the larger sheds until we realized what it really was: no more than a shell placed over what appeared to be an old antique shop. It seems that most of the sheds we saw were actually covers for other small stores or one-room homes - no longer occupied - remnants of an old town that this woman's father built many years in the past. The sheds were to deter curiosity seekers and, in this woman's case, would-be thieves. In her shop, there was an amazing collection of what seemed to me rare and valuable antiques. When we came through the front door, we saw a beautifully preserved sixteenth-century ivory pipe, hanging from a hook as if it were no more than a random piece of decor. The shop was filled with an amazing array of oddities and items: stone-aged spears and arrow heads, furniture from the old West in pristine condition, Civil War relics, old gold and silver coins and Chinese petition curtains that dated from some long ago dynasty known only to the most informed historian. The list went on and on, and this elderly woman – whose name we never learned, nor did she ask us ours – was a very trusting soul. She knew nothing of us, what type of men we were, but she had enough faith in her instincts to know we held no evil in our hearts. She lived there all alone in this store that her father opened after the town became no more than a roadside attraction. She said folks had moved out when the highway, built up and away from the town, stopped people from having a reason to drive through any longer. At highway speeds, the small town was no more than a blur, not even found on any map. She welcomed us as visitors, no questions asked. Heaven had a place for her when her time came to go home, of that I'm sure.

After a few hours of small talk and coffee, I excused myself to get some air. I stood outside the woman's shop with my back to Route 80 on the outskirts of her town, looking south. It was miles of open desert with a line of mountains in the distance. Below the mountains, running east to west across the entire horizon was a single line of train cars, and as with the train I saw in Montana I tried counting how many cars there were, but the heat distorted any clear view. I do recall that I stood there for a while and the line never seemed to end, just as it did when I was with Jayson atop the Silver Staircase Falls. This past year was only an instant in time (*the engine, second car, third car*), months of new experiences, new friends and old pain (*seventeen, eighteen, nineteen*) and I tried in vain to discover inside if it had been for the better or was it only a distraction (*twenty-nine, thirty...I lost count here*) from the real issue of me being me.

I thought if I ran I could make that train; I was certain I could. I'd hop a freight and leave Ray to fend for himself, live a new adventure, a life like Woody Guthrie did, traveling here and there, standing up for the persecuted, the ones done wrong by the self-serving righteous. But I was a coward and was too accustomed to living with a plan, comfortable with a formula I understood. I was unaware that would change soon enough.

One of the buildings was a small shed which was actually the shell for an old garage, a redundancy in structure for sure, but it served our purpose. Ray took apart my motorcycle inside to find what was wrong: a quarter-sized hole in one of the pistons. It had to be replaced, so with no choice we doubled-up on his small 250cc Suzuki and rode the twenty-six miles to Battle Mountain. We knew there was little hope that we could find what we needed, but not trying would have been more foolish. We rode back empty-handed with no idea what we were going to do.

It was decision time, and that night I came to one. I would hitch-hike the remaining 2,500 miles to New Jersey while Ray continued on with his bike. We knew his small 250cc would never survive the both of us that distance, or even half as far. The next morning, after a night of sleep in the garage where I left my bike, we said our goodbyes to the kindly woman, mayor of no one in this forgotten town. Soon I was up on Route 80, watching as Ray drove off into the distance, disappearing over the horizon. There I stood, alone under the morning desert sun, with the hiking frame from my bike on my back. Our elderly friend watched me for a short time until she returned to her home, waving one last goodbye. There were no cars in sight, and I had to wonder what the plan was now for me, what cruel fate put me here, or, more likely, what the hell I had gotten myself into?

It was official: I was off on a new adventure. The man who lived by a plan was now without one, this time solo, and diving into completely unfamiliar waters. "Hannah," I whispered to no one, "maybe I wouldn't be here if you…". My longing for a lost love was becoming a blame game. I put it on her that I was now a flea on the back of this dog called my existence. *Thanks for this, Hannah*, I thought bitterly. *Thanks for putting me here in the middle of nowhere so utterly alone.* But maybe I wasn't alone. If Hannah existed in my memories and in my thoughts, then surely that was some sort of companionship. Or was I desperately clinging to the reality of keeping my head together, my feet on the ground? I was in the middle of the Nevada desert, alone, at the beginning of a long leg of this journey and the prospect of getting back to New Jersey any time soon was a distant hope.

\* \* \*

It seemed like hours between passing cars and even longer until my first ride. My thumb ride journey took me a little more than one week to get back to New Jersey. Along the way, I met all sorts of people. There were gay men thinking I was an easy pick-up, middle-aged or older women who thought the same thing, lonely folks who just wanted an ear to bend along the highway of life. But for the most part, there were strangers who gave me a ride out of nothing more than kindness.

The first lift was from two girls in a pickup truck. Both were very friendly, and it was easy to label them as "flower children," wearing clothes that defined them as belonging to the peace and love generation now a few years past. The cab of their truck was lined with beads and peace signs and smelled of patchouli. I enjoyed their company, and they seemed to like hearing about my adventures through Big Sur and the mystery town I just left.

After a few hours of being on the road, they stopped to pick up another wayfarer with his thumb out. He was a strange one with long, straggly hair and a thick beard, wearing a bandana as a headband and thick horn-rimmed glasses. He was very hyper and appeared to be nervous, or maybe edgy, when he spoke. I offered to sit in the back of their pickup with him because the cab could hold only three, but the girls pleaded with me to stay with them and let him ride solo. Our new friend sat in the open truck bed chewing gum at a furious pace and swaying back and forth where he sat as we drove down the highway. He was obviously strung out on something; my guess was some form of speed.

Since the cab was tight even with only three people in it, I did ride in the back with him when we drove through the Salt Flats of Utah at night. Mostly I just wanted the experience. Despite our nervous guests' incessant, inane jabbering, I took notice that the night sky displayed even more stars than I saw in Big Sur and the desert's night air was sweet with what I imagined was the land cooling down, sighing in relief after so many hours of harsh sun. We pulled over for the night on the southern shore of the Great Salt Lake. Our speed freak friend seemed excited and kept telling me that we were going to get laid that night. Of course it never happened. Just out of sheer respect for their generosity, I would never try to be so bold and secondly, I was certain they weren't interested. It was hot and uncomfortably humid where we slept, and it stunk of industrial odor. On the opposite shore of the lake, I could see tall factory chimneys spewing their toxic waste into the atmosphere as gray-white smoke.

The following morning our jumpy, gum-chewing friend was gone. Guess he was unhappy with the turn of events the night before. The girls drove me to the eastern outskirts of Salt Lake City and gave me a string of beads to wear for good luck. I thanked them and again stuck out my thumb, waiting for my next ride. A Utah state trooper on the opposite side of Route 80 yelled via his car's loudspeaker that hitching a ride on the highway was illegal and I had to get off the road. Fortunately, I was near an entrance ramp and walked to the bottom, but there was very little traffic and the prospects of me getting a ride anytime soon from that location seemed grim. If there was a car every thirty minutes, I was lucky, but no one would stop. After who knows how long, rather than stand, I sat on my backpack and stuck my thumb out with each vehicle that passed. *This is getting depressing*, I thought before turning my mind to what other alternatives I had. That was when Topper Plentfull showed up.

* * *

Topper lived in Salt Lake City with his girlfriend. He was a bit older than me, maybe in his late twenties, with long, blond hair in a ponytail and Hollywood looks. He seemed like a smart enough guy, friendly and outgoing; but that isn't what I remember the most about Topper.

He drove a mint condition 1952 Chevy pickup truck that he had named "Louise." This was his pride-and-joy, and I recall it was impressive, but I also remember he was so particular, so overzealous of his truck that there was even a certain way - per his instructions - I had to get in and out of Louise. After he picked me up, we drove for maybe thirty minutes on Route 80 when he needed to find a car wash, the do-it-yourself kind. He was so meticulous in cleaning his truck it was not to be believed. Soon after leaving the car wash, we pulled into a small town to find a garage that gave Louise a tune-up and an oil change.

Back on the road, we drove south into Colorado, getting off of Route 80 and into the Rocky Mountains National Park via Route 40. Topper took a road that brought us high into the mountains. We pulled over to stop by a country store, a classic log cabin structure that served as a store, deli, and tourist info center. It was cold, and we seemed to be at about the beginning of the snow line. The incredible view from there included eagles flying *below* us. I wasn't prepared for this weather, wearing only shorts and a light windbreaker pullover.

While Topper ran into the store, I waited outside, leaning against the cabin by a window. I heard a buzzing noise to my left. Thinking it was a large insect; I quickly turned and discovered it was a hummingbird taking liquid from a bird feeder that hung on the window's side. Normally a hummingbird looks like a dragon fly because they fly so fast it's hard to get a visual, at least, that had been my experience with them in California; but this one, for a few moments, hovered inches from my face. Its wings were a complete blur while its greenish-blue body remained perfectly still, all the while keeping a watchful eye on me while it fed. Before I could blink, it vanished at an incredible speed. Fortune or good luck, whatever it was, allowed me to be there at just that moment to witness up close one of Nature's wonders, cast indelibly as one of my life's experiences. Emily Dickenson wrote a beautiful poem about the hummingbird: "*Within my Garden, rides a Bird / Upon a single Wheel – Whose spokes a dizzy Music make / As 'twere a travelling Mill*". How this wonderful creation found me no threat while it sought sustenance was a peaceful, rare experience. I envied its freedom, its ability to disappear in the blink of an eye leaving only the residue of a memory. If only I had that ability...

I was brought back to planet Earth by Topper's tap on my shoulder, letting me know he got what he needed. I wanted to tell him of my experience with the Hummingbird but Topper was cold and silent. I sensed my welcome was wearing out. Leaving the cabin store, we drove down from the mountains and continued east. The day was drawing to an end, so Topper said he would take me a bit further the next day but for now he thought it best we find a place to sleep for the night. He pulled into a clearing near the Colorado River where we could set up camp. Topper made sure he pulled deep into the clearing, far from the road, and we laid out our sleeping bags nearby among some high grass. It was that or sleep on stone or gravel, and my sleeping bag was thin and very old, so I thought it a good idea at the time. We didn't start a campfire because where we pulled over for the night might have been private property, and a fire would have drawn attention to us.

As the sun went down, the air began to cool, but it was still comfortable. I was very tired from our long day and fell asleep easily. Several hours later, nearer to the morning than the hour we turned in, I woke up shivering from the severe cold and damp air. I was wearing only shorts, a shirt, and a thin jacket, and the tall grass we lay in was soaking wet from dew and condensation from the nearby river. It was pitch black, and I could see Louise nearby but barely. Topper was fast asleep, and I wanted to wake him to ask if I could sleep in the truck, but I knew that would be a hard no because of the way he treated his Louise. With no option available in the darkness, I shivered from the unmerciful cold and decided it best to just force myself back to sleep. With my teeth chattering, my body curled into a fetal position and my hands between my thighs, I finally dozed off.

That night I dreamt of a time when Hannah and I fell asleep on the floor atop a blanket at the house of a friend of hers. How we got there, I don't remember, but I do recall it was an old house with several girls living together. One of Hannah's friends, Lorna, was there too. She spent the night calling me every name in the book because just a few nights earlier, on a night that my car sat at home with a dead battery, she had given me a ride home from The Ironclad. There was no way to stay with Hannah without a car. When I went to give Lorna a kiss on the cheek as thanks, she turned her head and made it a passionate lip-lock. I was taken by surprise and didn't react quickly enough, so she ended up believing there was something between us. She even went and told Hannah, which caused Hannah and I to spend the next night in my car, now with a new battery, parked by her house with Hannah telling me I should forget her and go with Lorna or Mary. Hours I spent trying to convince her of the truth: that the kiss was not planned and it was she that I wanted to be with. It must have worked because this night on that floor we lay prone on the blanket, her in my arms, and it didn't faze her in the least what Lorna said about me. Eventually Lorna left, and we were alone, lying together. Sleep came quickly enough, and we woke up just before the sun rose so I was able to get her home in time before her father returned from work. In my dream I didn't take Hannah home, she always stayed by my side...but only in my dreams.

When I woke this time, it was years later and I was in Colorado having spent the night sleeping next to a total stranger. The rising sun warmed the air fairly quickly. Though it was still cold, it wasn't nearly as cold as it had been during the night. I didn't mention my night-time predicament to Topper because I figured he wouldn't have cared in any case. I washed up in the nearby river, and we were soon back on the road.

Topper took a highway north through Colorado to get us back to Route 80 somewhere near the Wyoming-Nebraska border. In Nebraska, we paid a visit to the parents of one of his friends. They lived on a ranch with a good amount of land and were the first people I ever met that actually owned horses. These folks were real Westerners, evident by the decor of their home, fully regaled in Western paraphernalia. What was the most impressive aspect was the large Native American arrow and spearhead collection they possessed. The entire collection was mounted behind glass in several large frames hanging on their living and dining room walls and in their hallway. What was more amazing was that they said they found each piece of this marvelous collection on their land, and their land, from their front porch, stretched as far as I could see. I felt like someone out of a John Ford Western movie, except with my long hair and beads, I would have been an 'Injun' which maybe wasn't so far from the truth, according to my mother. She told me there was Native American blood on her father's side, though I was never able to find any proof.

After a brief visit, we said our goodbyes and hit the road. Topper drove me east for another few hours and dropped me off not near anything that I can recall except for an overpass. I think he just wanted to get rid of me, and I offered no argument. Since I was still so tired from so little sleep the night before and it was a hot day, I decided to grab some sleep in the shade of the overpass before I attempted to hitch another ride. Lighting up a joint was the order of the day, and I was grateful to have held on to a few since leaving Oakland. I smoked more than I should have, as was usual with me. I found an imaginary friend to talk to. He didn't have a name, didn't need one, and quite understood my plight, laughing at my jokes and choking back the tears when I expelled my tale of lost love. It wasn't long before my friend faded away, and I followed shortly after.

I woke up some time later to a buzzing sound, only this time it wasn't a Hummingbird, and it wasn't my imaginary friend: it was bees! Hundreds of them, maybe thousands, on me, on my backpack behind me, everywhere. I jumped up swinging my arms wildly and I ran. I don't remember how far, but I know it was fast. I stopped when I was certain there weren't any bees chasing or still on me, and how I wasn't bitten or stung countless times was a miracle in itself. Walking back slowly, I could see a small swarm still hovering over my pack. Through very slow, careful movements, great trepidation, and a long stick, I was able to get my backpack by tossing handfuls of sand, running, tossing, running, until I was able to snatch my pack and head to safer havens. Round two of nature and me, only this time I was the victor.

Afterwards I was able to manage a few short rides, one from a large, burly man in an old Chevette. He combed his hair into a greasy 1950s style DA, and he kept staring at my crotch while he was driving. He never propositioned me, but just the same I kept my hand in my backpack and on my hunting knife. Rules of the road. He needed to make a phone call and pulled off the highway to use a phone booth. While he was on the phone, he kept looking into the car and I got the distinct impression that he was talking about me. This was more than I could handle. I didn't want to become a statistic, so I got out, thanked him for the ride, and walked away. He drove alongside me, saying he could take me further, but I said no thanks and made it a point of having him notice my knife. He sped off in apparent anger.

Not knowing what to expect, I walked down a nearby dirt road and hung in the shade of a few trees not visible from the road just in case that maniac decided to circle back. After an hour or more, I walked back out to the highway and resumed my thumb ride journey, but I kept my eyes on both horizons for his car. It was later in the day and the sun was beginning to dip below the distant mountains. My prospects for another ride this day were slim.

\* \* \*

While I was living in California, at least for the first several months, I wanted to be alone. But did I really? Being alone was really my delving into a self-indulgent piteous display of mourning. The most somber times for me occurred at dusk, and those were particularly enhanced out here in the vast expanse of western skies. When the sun dipped just below the distant mountains and it's fading glimmer highlighted the horizon from one end to the other, diluting the last blue light of the day with the darkening warm colors of the spectrum...that was when I was at my loneliest, that was when I missed my Hannah the most. In the last rays of the sun's dying gleam I found both hope and despair:

conflicting but very active emotions inside. A part of me knew she was gone forever but hope held on, and I think at those moments hope felt alive, ever so dimly inside, that there was someone up there to hear my pleas, my prayers. Rebellion against a God Almighty did not exist at sunset when I needed someone, anyone, to understand me and the turmoil inside that was slowly draining my spirit. Tired and hungry, I decided to find a place to sleep and try for a ride again in the morning. I walked back down the dirt road and found a safe place under a tree near a wooden fence. I dreamt of Shelly that night. We were back in my parent's house the day she ended us but this time I just laughed and told her she wasn't nearly the woman that Hannah was.

# Chapter Ten
# Miguel

My next ride was my next-to-last ride before New Jersey. It was a camper with six people inside. Like Topper, they all appeared a few years older than me, and one in particular, name of Miguel, seemed to be the leader of their little group. Miguel appeared to be in his early 30s, stocky, maybe about my height of nearly six feet, with black, curly hair. I guessed he was Latino. He gave instructions to someone to get me something to drink and another to find me something to eat. They respected him. It was obvious in the upbeat atmosphere of their gathering that they were more than happy to oblige whatever Miguel wanted done. He projected warmth that made you feel you could trust him and he had your back. The camper was stockpiled with living paraphernalia; I could tell it had been used to a great extent, and just like my Dodge van, the roof was loaded with boxes covered by a tarpaulin stretched tight and tied down over the whole load.

"Where is your journey taking you to, amigo?" Miguel asked.

"New Jersey" I replied, rather awkwardly. Strange how I sounded embarrassed to say that was my destination.

"Why?" was his next question. Some of the people in his little soiree laughed, but I'm betting that probably a lot of folk would have asked the same question. I explained I was going back home after living in California for a year. It was easy to immediately discern Miguel was a serious, thoughtful individual. He accepted my simple explanation and left it at that.

"Boothbay Harbor in Maine is where we intend to land, and hang there till the fall colors are spread over the landscape", Miquel explained.

I learned they'd been on the road for almost two years just travelling around, finding a small town or village to settle in for a short stay to make some money before hitting the road again. Miguel said their driver, Butch, owned the camper and was a master mechanic who kept it running all this time. Another great mechanic in my life: made me think of how different these circumstances might have been if Mike made the trip west.

Butch, listening to what Miguel was telling me, turned his head slightly toward us while keeping his eyes on the road and said:

"Third engine so far and just replaced the rear axle, but this momma won't die." At least he didn't give it a name, like Topper's Louise.

Jimi Hendrix's *Electric Ladyland* album was blasting out of an eight-track player the camper had built into a cabinet by the back doors. Miguel asked someone to please turn it down a bit so it would be easier to talk. He said they had planned on stopping soon for the night and if I wanted to I could stay with them and they could drive me further east tomorrow.

"Sure, why not?" I responded. It wasn't like I was in a rush to get to where I was going. It was so tempting to ask if I could join them in their Maine trip, but as it was they were pressed for room with six people already, and I didn't want to impose.

We pulled into a rest area for trucks that allowed overnight parking. Miguel told Butch to park at the far end of the lot, by the trees and picnic tables so we would be out of the way of others. Once we parked, everyone had a chore, and methodically they unloaded camping equipment and got a fire going on one of the picnic area's metal grills. From a storage space beneath the camper, they pulled out lawn chairs, a few of them recliners, one of which Miguel insisted I use for the night. Everything they owned had seen better days, and Miguel explained that most of what they had was what they scrounged from people's trash or purchased for a few dollars from garage or yard sales. Such a unique group, living the Ken Kesey lifestyle to a greater extent than I first realized.

After a hearty meal of grilled eggplant and squash, washed down with cold beer, I settled back in the recliner they gave me and was once again beneath a blanket of stars, a vision I knew was coming to a close because back in the part of New Jersey where I was from there hasn't been a blanket of stars visible since maybe the 1800s. Miguel pulled his recliner up next to mine and offered me a dot of blotter acid. He said it was a good night to travel, and I agreed, placing the small paper under my tongue.

It wasn't long before my journey began. The grass around me started to sway back and forth, as if caught in a whirling dervish moving at a gracefully slow pace. The trunks of the trees nearby seemed to crystallize with glistening points of light. I was enjoying this trip. My head was in a good place; even thinking of Hannah wasn't bringing me down. At one point, I envisioned her in full clarity over by the fire, stoking the dying flames back into life, then coming towards us from the metal grill, and in my delusional state, I stood up to clarify what I was looking at. It was one of the women in Miguel's group who didn't come close to resembling Hannah. I watched in awe as she slowly morphed into someone I never met.

As I sat back down, Miguel unexpectedly asked:

"Why are you *really* going back? I can sense there is a battle in your soul, but if you don't want to talk about it, that's cool."

Don't ask me why, but Miguel became the only person in my entire life to whom I told the story of Hannah and Shelly. I explained how after four years and several girlfriends since, including being married, I couldn't quit this woman that I was with for only three months. All the details came out, how Hannah became Shelly to my friends because of my fear of scorn and ridicule, how I would drive past her house or park nearby but was always too frightened to ring her doorbell. I told him I wrote to both women from California, but Hannah never wrote back and, now, having to return to New Jersey out of necessity, I wasn't sure what lay ahead for me being so close to Hannah with no recourse of being with her. I told him that at least living in California a few thousand miles away I had an excuse, that the great distance prevented me from seeing her again.

Miguel asked, "Do you know what she's up to now? Is she still living home? Is she married?"

"No, I don't have any idea where or how she is" was my reply. I didn't really have any answers, since Hannah and I had no common friends I had no one to ask about her. Miguel laid back in his recliner, becoming quiet and pensive as he stared at the starry ceiling for a short time before he spoke. He told me he served two tours in Vietnam in the late 1960s and how near the end of his first tour he received word from home that his sweetheart Madeline, the girl that he'd been with since grammar school and had planned to marry, died in a car crash. He said she was a passenger in the vehicle of one of Miguel's high school buddies named Bill and they were drinking. They tried to beat the gates at a train crossing but didn't make it. His sergeant told him the Army was sending him home on an early discharge since he had only a month left on his first tour, but he refused to go. Miguel said by the time he got back she would be buried and he could grieve just as easily in Vietnam as he could back home. The Army told him they don't need distracted soldiers in the field who couldn't concentrate on the task at hand; others would be at risk, but Miguel insisted he would be okay. The Army put him through a battery of psych tests to be sure before they approved his being reinstated. After that, Miguel signed on for his second tour.

I had to ask, "Why? Why wouldn't you go home? What about your family, her family?"

"Lost my father when I was very young," Miguel explained, "my Mom remarried and had little time for me once she began having a new family to attend to. Was raised by my grandmother who died before I left for 'Nam. I have a brother and two sisters I've only met a few times."

He then told me that, in Madeline's letters, she was writing more and more about Bill and how comforting he was as a good friend while Miguel was away. It wasn't hard to figure out what was going on, so when the news came of her death and how she died with Bill at the wheel, it was almost as if life was giving him a Dear John letter. He was heartbroken, but soldiering taught him how to separate his emotions from what he was assigned to do. He said he wasn't a proponent of the war, had seen how useless the decimation had been, especially to the indigenous peoples there, but he was drafted with no way out.

How petty I felt then, how small my overused and trivial lost love bit seemed to be now compared to Miguel's story. At least, as far as I hoped, Hannah was living her life back east. Even if she was with someone, which was a safe bet, I knew that she had her feet planted on this good earth. Miguel seemed to sense how I felt, and he told me everyone's story is their own and that it's what it means to them inside that counts, no matter the external circumstances or what others may think.

"I'm running way, amigo," Miguel said softly, "running from home and Madeline's memory. Traveling with these good folk gives me purpose, gives me a reason to keep on keeping on. I know I can't go home".

He never mentioned where home was. I never asked, but it didn't escape me how similar our reasons were for not wanting to be home. We both lost a love we cherished and distance seemed the only logical course to take. Only difference was I was heading back into the abyss while Miguel was keeping a good deal of miles between him and what he was running from.

It was a beautiful, tranquil evening. Miguel's story mellowed my trip down, and I admired the volume of stars in the moonless sky. Thought about my life and what compelled me on the path I was taking. On impulse I pulled my flute from my backpack. Miquel's eyes opened wide with excitement:

"*Mi amigo*", he said, "It would be a wonderful trip if you could give us some sweet sounds right now".

"It's the least I can do." I told him and proceeded to blow out some soft, soothing melodies. One of the women from his group joined us carrying a wooden Plains flute with a resounding tonality I had never experienced until that moment: a lilting, all-encompassing, sweet dirge-like tenor that one felt as well as heard. Together we merged musically, complementing each other's offerings and cadences to the evening spirits. I can't tell you if it was due to the blotter acid but what she and I produced that night was the nearest I got to getting religion in quite some time. When we were done, due to exhaustion more than anything else, Miquel and the rest of his group applauded our work.

"Amazing, man", Miquel said, "thank you so much for that".

I replied it was my pleasure, put my flute away and felt my body fading into the depths of sleep. My eyes slowly closed, and I don't remember my dreams from that night.

The next morning, we were back on the road. After a few hours as we neared Chicago, Miguel said:

"This is where we'll let you off, my friend. A little side trip's in order for us before we head northeast to Maine."

I couldn't thank him and his friends enough. He let me have the top of a Styrofoam cooler that I could use as a sign. With a marker, Miguel wrote "NJ" on the cover. When they were about to exit the highway near Chicago, they pulled over and directed me to a large cloverleaf in the roadway with a long line of toll booths, telling me that was my best shot to get my next lift east. Before I left, we all passed around a joint. Butch said it was a celebration, a toast to our brief time together.

As I got out, Miguel leaned in to give me a hug and whispered in my ear:

"Don't ever let your dreams die, Cookie. They die easily enough on their own, and your job is to try and prevent that." We hugged, and they left, and I was alone.

\* \* \*

I walked to a spot on the side of the road near the toll booths, and before I stuck out my NJ sign, I took a seat on a guardrail. Getting stoned wasn't a good idea because now I was alone with my thoughts and once again alone in the world. It hit me that this was real: I was returning to New Jersey, and I was overwhelmed with anxiety. What had I accomplished in the past year? I hadn't escaped from anything, hadn't experienced a life-changing moment that made me a better man. I was still the me that left New Jersey the previous summer, and it was still (as far as I knew) where Hannah was but if I was a few miles away or an entire continent away, it made no difference. With no word from her or of her for so many years now: I was angry at myself that I couldn't relegate her to just a nice memory rather than a devastating loss. But there I was on the side of the road in Chicago, my entire worldly possessions on my back, still pining for a woman who probably forgot I even existed.

Soon I decided it was thumbs-out time. A lot of cars passed me by and beeped, but no one stopped. A carful of girls honked their horn and called me an asshole as they laughed and drove by. *Boy*, I thought, *Chicago people really suck.*

# Chapter Eleven
# "It's him! He's here!"

It was getting dark, and I was worried that I'd have to sleep on the side of the road somewhere and try again in the morning when there was more light. While I was considering this very possibility, a van stopped just before going through one of the cash-only lanes on the other side of the highway. A young man opened the van's side door and yelled to me to come over, shouting that he would give me a lift. I made my way through the many toll lanes to the van where I met Chris, formerly of Brooklyn but now living in Chicago, my most memorable ride. Chris informed me that I was standing on the westbound side of the highway with my NJ sign held out! I was so stoned I never realized it and would have stood there till dawn if he hadn't spotted me and U-turned back around to get me. We both got a good belly laugh over that one.

Chris was genuine, all-the-way Brooklyn, an absolutely vibrant persona, heavy Brooklyn accent right out of a Dead End Kids movie. He told me his family moved to Chicago when his father's job relocated there a few years ago and he hated it, fought like Mugsy from the Dead End kids with his old man to let him stay in Brooklyn, but it was to no avail. Chris was driving back to visit family and friends he hadn't seen since he left, said he had plans to live like a "New Yawker" for the next week and forget about Chicago. We shared the driving so he could get some sleep, and after a few hours, we pulled into a highway rest stop for some food. Chris lit up a joint before we went in (funny how most of my rides just assumed I would indulge in a bit of the weed if offered), and the effect was the spectacle we made inside. I remember sitting at the counter experiencing uncontrollable laughter over the idea of having a pet bird on a leash that would be good on a summer night when the air was thick with mosquitoes, since we assumed the bird would feast on the bothersome pests. The folks near us actually seemed to enjoy our absurd tangent. Back then, the world wasn't so uptight and hard-ass like it is now. It was a lot of fun, more free-spirited; the conservative agenda that engulfed America soon afterwards hadn't arrived yet.

Chris was behind the wheel when we crossed over the Delaware Water Gap. I could see the *Welcome to New Jersey* sign on the highway, and the reality of the last year once again set in. My heart was beating hard in my chest from anxiety. When the New York City skyline came into view, Chris began to hoot and holler; he was ecstatic to be near the end of his journey. How I so wished I felt what he was feeling just then; instead, I wondered if he noticed how I withdrew into myself. He dropped me off at the Route 17 southbound ramp in Hasbrouck Heights, where we said our goodbyes. To this day, I am disappointed that I did not get his address; he was real good people, one of the most dynamic personalities I ever met, and it would have been so cool to have stayed in touch with him.

\* \* \*

Slowly I walked down the ramp and crossed over Route 17 to hitch a ride south. Standing near the highway, I was actually considering walking back up the ramp to Route 80's west bound lanes and putting out my thumb for a ride back to Jayson in California. All the old insecurities came rushing back; all the emotions I left New Jersey to escape were there. My heart was still broken; my world would once again consist of emptiness and people who would call me friend but about whom I had my doubts. I was no more than a few miles from Hannah's house, and just a few weeks earlier I had been over 2,000 miles from her front door, but the pain was the same, no matter the distance.

My very last ride was a young lady with dyed blonde hair who wore heavy eyeliner and makeup. She said she was from Lodi. Like Chris personified Brooklyn, this girl was Jersey with a capital J: gum-smacking, and talking about clubbing and that it must have been cool to hitch across the country and that someday she was planning on traveling yak, yak, yak. While she drove and yapped, I just stared out the window at the fast food places, the gas stations, and the diners that lined Route 17, wondering what kind of life this girl was living the past year while I was in California? Just a fleeting thought, though; I really didn't care.

The last mile was on foot. I walked down the hill to my parents' house, and my mother happened to be walking up the block.

"It's him! he's here!" she yelled to my father, who was with my Uncle Bill in the backyard of their home.

*It's him, all right*, I thought, *only the man they remember is not the man who came back.* I returned less of the man I wanted to be, more worldly through experience, but less intuitive toward the ways of living because I had taken in too much information in the last year and didn't know how to process it into something useful. My soul was vacant. California had failed me, I had failed me. It was back to Jersey living, but *living* was a veiled description because I was again in the throes of all the agony that drove me from here in the all-too-recent past. Living in a vacuum would be an ample description. It was late August, 1975. I had been gone just over a year, but it might as well have been a day. I left with a van packed full of the items that make up a person's life and came back with nothing more than the clothes on my back and a backpack that contained the few things I had left in this world.

\* \* \*

Adjusting to New Jersey life again was one of the most difficult transitions I ever had to make. My friends, particularly Pat, were happy I was back but they would occasionally comment that I'd become a more serious individual from the open, outgoing man they remember. I lost that man, somewhere at a curve in the road, next to a train track, in an old, abandoned town, near an overpass, at a tollbooth in Chicago, was always my reply but they never understood. How much more confusing would it have been if I told them the me that was me was stolen a long time ago by a woman from Hackensack and that the me they remember was never coming back. It was time to move on despite the inner turmoil I was dealing with.

Ray? Turns out his bike died somewhere in Pennsylvania, and he got a job on a farm for a few days to earn a few bucks. He hitched from there, and a week after my arrival, he showed up and moved into my parents' house with me, living in the basement. It was a move a lot of people came to regret. Especially me. He was a very devious and unreliable individual who at first charmed my friends as he did me but soon enough alienated each and every one of them, including my parents. Ray was gone again to parts unknown within a few months.

I never attempted to contact Hannah after I got back, though the temptation was there. If I could admit anything, it would be that I borrowed a friend's car just a few days after my return and made what was to become my last drive-by past her house in Hackensack. Again I didn't stop, and no one was out front. If and when it ever came up among friends, I continued to mourn the loss of Shelly when it meant Hannah, though by now no one ever asked any longer. If nothing else, my arduous trek hardened me to any further open displays of grief, but I continued to live the lie. I had returned to the dismal swamps of New Jersey, or, more likely, it had sucked me back in. I knew that this time it was for keeps.

**The Year behind Me**
**2011**

- *Singer Amy Winehouse dies*

- *Arizona Congresswoman Gabrielle Giffords was shot along with twelve others while making a public appearance in Tucson by accused gunman Jared Loughner. Six of the people who were shot die, one of dead was a nine year old girl. Giffords survived the attack but was in critical condition*

- *Average cost of a gallon of gas: $3.52*

- *North Korea's Kim Jong Il dies and is replaced by his song Kim Jong Un*

- *Adele's "21" is named top cd of the year by Rolling Stone*

- *Steve Jobs, co-founder of Apple, dies*

- *Apple releases the iPhone 4S on October 14th, only nine days after the death of co-founder Steve Jobs.*

- *Forty years and one month later I meet Hannah again...for the last time.*

# Epilogue
# The Lie Resolved

*Fourteen thousand, six hundred and*
*thirty days. So long ago when the magic*
*was there but the magician was not, when*
*the music was there but the musician was not.*

It was forty years and one month from the last time I saw Hannah until I saw her again. In a supermarket near where I live and frequently shop, I noticed a young lady working there who, except for being a brunette, was a young Hannah to a fault. The onslaught of time, having a family and a career, and just life's way of racing by had put Hannah into the deepest recesses of my memory, but seeing this young girl who was the image of Hannah brought out a curiosity that I had to fulfill. Social networking was the tool I used to locate her. Typing in *Hannah* along with her maiden name brought me to a page that displayed her image along with her married name. It was easy enough to recognize the now older woman on my computer: still beautiful with those baby blues staring out at the world. Over a period of months, I would bring up her page just to feel that thrill of discovery, locating the woman who brought me love, heartache, and adventure assembled in so many pixels on the screen of my PC's monitor. There was no sudden impulse to contact her. I had moved on many, many years ago, married now to a wonderful woman named Mattie who gave me four beautiful children. But still there was that excitement, the wonder of "what if" that never leaves you when you think of someone in your life you loved early on.

On July 1st, 2011, I decided to give it a shot and sent a message to Hannah asking if she was indeed the same Hannah from Hackensack, New Jersey. More than two months went by with no reply, and I assumed once again she just wasn't interested in re-establishing contact with me. I will admit I was disappointed, checking my inbox from time to time and finding nothing. Youth has a habit of always reminding you how it's been left in the past for others to experience, and this was one of those reminders, but life lived long enough recycles itself in mysterious ways. September 8th, 2011, I received a message from Hannah. It simply read: "Is this the same man who called his girlfriend Mary by my name, not once, but twice?"

There is nothing I can say to accurately describe how I felt, simply that I was very happy should suffice. We began exchanging messages for a day or two but then decided to talk on the phone because there was too much catching up to do to write it all out. I nervously dialed her cell phone, feeling a torrent of emotions, not knowing what to expect. After two rings, Hannah answered. Her voice was different than what I remembered, but her slight Scottish accent and way of putting words together was still unmistakably Hannah. I learned she was a retired nurse, had two boys, and had married a good man named Ted when she was 34. I told her about Carrie-ann and Mattie, my children who were all adults now, and that I too was retired, though not by choice. She asked me questions about my time in California, and I told her what I could remember, but I never revealed to her why I left New Jersey to begin with, never told her how many times during the course of that year she was by my side, though only in my imagination, only in my prayers, and how, when the moon was full, I would whisper her name.

I learned both her parents had passed on, and she was consoling when I informed her I lost Mom just a short time ago but was glad that Dad was still around, living upstairs from me and Mattie. Hannah had been engaged a few times before meeting Ted, and he turned her life around, giving her the stability she hadn't had before. She understood when I explained Pat wasn't in my life any longer and hadn't been for some time. It saddened her to hear of Mike's passing. Hannah laughed and called me a player when I told her that coincidentally Mary and I had just been in contact with each other.

The biggest surprise, or revelation, of our discussion came when we began talking about what happened to us back then. After forty years and one month, I finally got the chance to reveal what my feelings for her were when we were both so young. I explained that I had never been able to express them because I had just had my heart broken by Shelly only a few months before we met, because I was with Mary, but mostly because I sensed she considered me just a guy she was dating and no one to get serious with. I told her that I adored her, that she was the most beautiful woman I ever met in my teenage years and that it took me quite some time to move past her memory…words I never believed I'd ever get to say.

There was a pause before Hannah replied, an almost why-did-I-tell-her-that silence. Again, I felt flushed, and foolish but what she said next was the very last thing I ever expected to hear on this earth: she explained that she had such a crush on me and was shattered when she got the call that my car died and I had no way to see her any longer, but she was just getting over a broken engagement and a devastating incident in her life that caused her to be cautious with men. Discretion prevented her from letting me know how much she cared for me. She said she thought I would be the *love of her life*, but I was there and gone so quickly. I learned she called my house at least two times after my last call, leaving messages with my mother, but they were messages I never received. Bobby James, she explained, was an attempt to have a lifeline to me after I left, as she figured I would be in touch with Bobby since I had been in the band with him. When I never came around, she said Bobby became a shoulder to lean on, and they ended up living together, but, no, she never loved him. And she never received the letter that I mailed from California, maybe because I didn't know her house number or even if I spelled her last name correctly. Had she gotten the letter, Hannah said, she would have seriously considered coming out west because she was between relationships then and I was always in her thoughts.

I never told her about my road trips to her neighborhood, driving by but never stopping. I didn't think that would go over well with what I now knew. My entire life, from 1971 to that moment, was suddenly framed in a new perspective. The lie I lived so long ago was enshrouded in a truth I hadn't even been aware of. I quickly imagined how different my story would have been had I been known of Hannah's feelings for me. Our lives are shaped by events that are supposed to happen - so I've been told - and only now was I beginning to realize that was a distinct possibility.

I asked her if there was any chance she still had the photo booth pictures from our carnival date. Hannah replied that she can't recall our being in the booth, much less still having the photos. But she did tell me of the fate of the stuffed dog I won for her that day: after our last phone conversation, she was so hurt and angry she threw it out, in so many pieces. She said she regretted that later on because it was the only thing she had to remember me by. Both of us expressed disappointment that there were no pictures of our time together so many years ago. I was surprised to hear how she would tell her boys when they were young the story of how she mistook the moon for a street lamp that night in the park. They would laugh each time when she told them how I mentioned it was indeed the moon.

We then came to a momentous decision: to meet somewhere because even the phone was insufficient to cover all those years apart, and the overwhelming curiosity and, yes, the excitement of seeing each other again was foremost in our decision. I discovered she lived near the "rock" and suggested an afternoon that I was free. This worked for her. We never told Ted or Mattie because we didn't want them to read into it as anything more than an innocent meeting between two old friends.

It was October 6th, 2011, a Thursday. The weather was perfect, sunshine and a few clouds gracing a deep blue sky. I arrived early, which was my usual mode of arriving anywhere. When it was getting past our meeting time, I began to anxiously wonder if maybe she had second thoughts until I saw her get out of her SUV in the parking lot and walk toward me. Forty years and one month disappeared in an instant. Like me, she was older. Her strawberry blonde hair was now all blond, and I had lost my long locks ages ago, sporting a bald look, but we both wore our years proudly, and she was still just as gorgeous as I remember. The smiles on our faces turned to laughter when we hugged; it was a moment in my life I never, ever dreamed would happen again, holding my Hannah in my arms. I could sense she felt the same way. The feeling of guilt and boundless joy enveloped me; the perception of being transported back to the parking lot at The Ironclad was overwhelming, but we weren't those kids anymore. The years had put so much time and distance between us, yet for that solitary hug my wish at the diner next to The Ironclad where I wanted time to stop was being fulfilled.

There was so much more to learn about each other, so we strolled through the park, oblivious to the world, and recapped our entire lives in just a few short hours. I told Hannah what I did with music after Bobby James, how I learned to play the flute. Told her about my Brattleboro, Vermont gig with Jayson and how with every note I played I could feel her with me. She told me she was proud of me, something I had hoped for so long ago after that beautiful night of music. I so wished she could have been there in body as well as spirit.

We both thought how fortunate we were to have Ted and Mattie and that watching our children grow up was the greatest joy we had in life. I told Hannah I thought I could never fall in love again after we parted, especially when being married to Carrie-ann did not deter my longing for her, but Mattie was a kindred soul who loved me for who I was and that made it easy to make a life with her. A short distance from the parking lot, we strolled over to our long-ago romantic setting of the rock. This time I sat while Hannah stood, leaning against me as we relived just briefly those moments from a time long since passed.

A group of people were passing by us on the trail when a woman came up to us and commented that we made such a cute couple and asked if we wanted her to take our picture together. We were taken aback by her request because she had no camera or phone visible and neither did we, so what motivated her to ask was a very curious thing. But I thought *what the hell.* I took out my phone and handed it to her. Hannah and I put our arms around each other, and the woman took our picture. We thanked her, and she joined her group further down the path. It is ironic that the only picture ever taken of Hannah and me together, other than the long-lost photo booth snapshots, was forty years and one month later and snapped by a total stranger. We must have radiated a blissful aura that she recognized, and it compelled her to offer us a chance to record that moment in eternity together.

The time passed so quickly and all too soon we were in the parking lot at our vehicles. This magical afternoon was ending, the sun was beginning to set and those hues on the horizon which so long ago represented both hope and despair to me were not as brilliant in their luster as I recalled. We were preparing to say goodbye. Hannah told me how incredible an experience this was, and I agreed, telling her it was for me too. Then there was a long moment of silence, an unexpected silence where we did nothing but look deeply into each other's eyes. This time, she didn't mind me staring. I was searching for the Hannah of my youth, and I'm sure she was searching for that boy in the doorway of The Ironclad but unlike that moment, she didn't turn her gaze away. There were no friends between us and no diner for me to court her at; no parking lot where two people so young shared their first kiss. There was just us, and we saw in each other's eyes all the years that had passed and all the "what ifs" that might have been if only we understood the truth of that time. We hugged again, tighter than before, and I whispered softly into her ear:

"Hannah…I'm so sorry."

She understood what I meant, lightly kissed my cheek, and left without another word. As she was walking back to her truck, I called out to her:

"Hannah," I said, "you're my girl."

"Always was," she replied. She smiled, gave me a small wave goodbye, got into her SUV, and drove away.

That was the last time I saw or spoke to Hannah. We couldn't be friends, though we might have wanted to, because friendship would have been a regression from the powerful emotion we shared that apparently stuck with us forty years and one month later. Did I want Hannah back in my life? Maybe I did but I was happy now, content with what was given me. It was too late to start over, we both already lived out most of our years and we both knew that what we now had was not something we were willing to give up. I watched her drive out of the park, and soon I was on the road home. Amazingly, *Birds* by Neil Young – now a song on the playlist of a classic rock station on my satellite radio – was playing, but I didn't keep it on. Didn't need to this time. I tuned into another station where *Starlight* by Muse was now enveloping my world. While Matthew Bellamy sang "*I just wanted to hold you here in my arms*" I adjusted my rear-view mirror, bringing into clearer focus the road behind me where I could see the red tail lights of Hannah's SUV disappearing in the opposite direction. I found myself immersed in the irony, and instead of tears, I felt joy, the joy of living a life that I just learned had not been lived in vain.

Printed in Great Britain
by Amazon